READINGS IN SRI AUROBINDO'S
REBIRTH AND KARMA

Santosh Krinsky

LOTUS PRESS

Twin Lakes, WI

Chapter Numbers and Titles follow the original text of *Rebirth and Karma*

Printed in the United States of America

ISBN: 978-0-9409-8508-7

Library of Congress Control Number: 2013908115

Printed In USA

Published by:

LOTUS
PRESS

Lotus Press
P.O. Box 325
Twin Lakes, WI 53181 USA
800-824-6396 (toll free order phone)
262-889-8561 (office phone)
262-889-2461 (office fax)
www.lotuspress.com (website)
lotuspress@lotuspress.com (email)

TABLE OF CONTENTS

Section II The Lines of Karma

Section III The Higher Lines of Karma

Appendices

DEDICATION AND ACKNOWLEDGEMENTS

I dedicate this book to Sri Aurobindo and the Mother, who have guided and blessed my life and seeking for all of my adult life.

I would like to acknowledge also a debt of gratitude to Sri M.P. Pandit, who taught by example and by his tremendous discipline and dedication to the yoga of Sri Aurobindo and the Mother. I was particularly inspired to follow the current book's format from his *Readings in Savitri* (10 volume set) which encouraged me to dedicate time regularly over a period of years to carry out the process of creating these readings.

I am grateful to my life-partner and wife Karuna who has been a support and inspiration to me with her quiet and dedicated efforts of sadhana, as well as to my two children Marina Mahati and Shanta Maya who challenged us to grow and expand our view of life as we raised and home-schooled them.

I have to also acknowledge the efforts of His Holiness, the XIV Dalai Lama, whose compassionate, caring and tireless efforts for building a world of peace, harmony and understanding have provided support and solace in a world filled with conflict and suffering.

FOREWORD

REBIRTH AND KARMA

Karma is a common word today that has entered into most of the languages of the world. Yet karma remains one of the most misunderstood of all subjects. Most people look at karma in a simplistic manner, as if what our karma brings to us was little more than rewards and punishments for our petty moralistic actions in life.

Another common approach to karma is to make it into a type of destiny, almost a 'my karma made me do it' scenario. Though karma means action, and refers to the effects of what we ourselves have done in the past, many people have the attitude that they are victims of their own karma and stand helpless before it. Karma can become an excuse as to why we have not done better in life, with the blame being shifted to others. 'After all it was my karma,' is often said, as if we have to accept being prevented from advancing in life because of something shadowing us from our past.

Rebirth or reincarnation, as it is also called, similarly is a topic of great mystery and confusion, though many people today accept it as true. A belief in rebirth or reincarnation is now common not only among Hindus and Buddhists who have this as part of their religions, but also among many New Age groups in the West, and even into the general population, extending to a number of Christians. Reincarnation has existed as an alternative view in western culture to the ideas of heaven and hell, even in the early days of Christianity. Now in an era of growing religious freedom, it is moving more out into the open.

There are several popular books and movies with stories of reincarnation, but little that explains rebirth in a cohesive, comprehensive and systematic manner, either as to its process or as to its rationale. It is often unclear who or what within us is reborn, or why rebirth might be necessary, though a vague idea of karma is frequently brought into the picture.

Karma and rebirth are two ideas that go together traditionally in Dharmic traditions like Hinduism and Buddhism. Karma implies rebirth, as the effects of our actions under the law of karma cannot be fully played out in a single life. Accepting the fact of rebirth turns our understanding of karma in a spiritual direction. It means that we take additional births because we have not yet worked out all our higher potentials in life, which means that karma can be a force for spiritual growth, not merely a type of divine justice.

Certainly if we look at the world around us, particularly at human society as we have known it historically, we do not see much of justice in the world. The bad generally prevails over the good. Evil often goes unpunished. Those who are good and kind often suffer tragedies in their lives. Good deeds are often rewarded with deceit, exploitation or harm. Violence often achieves its aim of worldly power and affluence. If there is a God or Divine power looking over the world, it does not seem to be much concerned about the sorrow of the world. Similarly, if there is a law of karma, it does not seem to reward us for our efforts to good, rather it seems to make our lives more difficult if we take to the spiritual path. However, if we understand karma as a process directing us to higher awareness, then we can see that more important than what happens to us outwardly is our ability to transcend it inwardly.

Sri Aurobindo has provided what may be the most comprehensive, cogent, clear and balanced view of karma and rebirth available. Though he was one of the greatest Yogis of all time, he has examined this complex topic in a clear and rational manner like a research scientist, and does not need to invoke any ultimate mystery or illusion to explain karma away. He has removed from the idea of karma the complications of religious moralism, or other subjective value judgments. He has rejected the negative idea of karma as mere inertia and reveals a Divine force behind it.

Aurobindo presents karma and rebirth relative to the evolution of consciousness as a kind of natural law, devoid of any judgmental retribution by any God or Divine agency. He shows that the purpose of karma and rebirth is not to give out worldly rewards and punishments but to help the soul develop a higher awareness, detachment, discrimination, and inner peace.

We find in the world of nature the existence an evolution of bodies, with ever more complex physical forms and nervous systems developing through time, with the human being culminating from eons of evolution through plants and animals. This

Darwinian approach, with various modifications, is widely accepted today. From the spiritual standpoint, the question arises as to whether there is any accompanying inner evolution of intelligence or consciousness, or whether this evolution simply arises from physical necessity. Science is yet debating this issue, but Yoga has long found its answer. It is a growth in consciousness the causes more sophisticated bodily forms to evolve.

Yoga in its true sense as the development of consciousness is the method for the higher evolution of consciousness in human beings. Sri Aurobindo notes:

"The true foundation of the theory of rebirth is the evolution of the soul, or rather its efflorescence out of the veil of Matter and its gradual self-finding."

"And if this gradual efflorescence be true, then the theory of rebirth is an intellectual necessity, a logically unavoidable corollary."

A seasoned mountain climber looks for more difficult slopes to climb and is not happy with walking on the comfortable level ground, where his capacities are not challenged. Similarly, the soul looks for lives that are challenging in terms of the evolution of consciousness, which cause it to ask fundamental questions and stimulate it look within, rather than lives that allow it to simply enjoy outer happiness or avoid outer sorrow.

Disparities in birth can reflect different powers of the soul, rather than punishment on those who may have difficulties in life. Even great gurus and avatars have had to suffer from many forms of human iniquity such as we find in the lives of Rama, Krishna, Jesus, and even Sri Aurobindo himself. Having a Divine presence within oneself allows one to overcome outer difficulties, it does not prevent us from experiencing these. The greatest strength is to be able to over come all difficulties by the power of awareness, not the ability to avoid them, which is impossible in this world build on opposition and duality.

What then is the evolution of consciousness? Consciousness in its pure essence is unchangeable and immutable. It is the Self of all and the Universal Being. What evolves is the instrumentality of consciousness, which in the case of human beings is the mind. However, if we look at the human mind carefully we see that it is an inferior vehicle for the full manifestation of consciousness. The mind reflects, as even modern psychology knows, more of the unconscious. Much of what we call our consciousness is a subconscious process, a series of reactions, almost mechanical in nature, tied to instinct, emotion and physical habits. We have our buttons as we all well know that others can easily push to get us to do what they want. These tendencies are our karmic patterns or samskaras in Sanskrit.

The evolution of consciousness requires a higher evolution of the mind, if not the evolution of a higher vehicle than the mind as we know it, what Sri Aurobindo calls the Supermind. The soul is evolving through rebirth towards Self-realization and union with the Divine by learning how to exceed the karmic limitations of the mind. This can lead us to a new stage in evolution in which a higher type of being can manifest in this physical world.

Sri Aurobindo's discussion of Karma and Rebirth helps us answer the most vexing questions of "Why is there suffering in the world?" and "Why is there evil" and how we can overcome these. It explains the natural and divine necessity of karma in the unfoldment of the universe.

As in his previous books of readings in Sri Aurobindo, Santosh Krinsky has taken the primary points of Sri Aurobindo's understanding, explained and highlighted them for the modern reader to more easily understand. The breadth of Aurobindo's thought is difficult for those of us today with limited attention spans and limited time. Krinsky shows the essence of Aurobindo's transformative message so that we can benefit from its core truth.

Anyone who appreciates the law of karma or entertains some possibility of rebirth or reincarnation would benefit from reading this book – and even those who might find karma and rebirth to be irrational would also benefit.

David Frawley (Vamadeva Shastri)
Author, Soma in Yoga and Ayurveda, Mantra Yoga and Primal Sound
Director, American Institute of Vedic Studies (www.vedanet.com)

INTRODUCTION

Introduction to Sri Aurobindo's *Rebirth and Karma*

The entire question of rebirth, sometimes called reincarnation, is shrouded in religious dogma, philosophical argument and rampant popular superstition. It is therefore extremely difficult to understand what in fact the situation is–is there some form of rebirth? If so, what is the functioning, mechanism and purpose of rebirth? How do we ascertain the facts relating to the operation of the process of rebirth? Is there any way to verify, one way or the other, the reality of rebirth?

Whether or not rebirth is a reality, there is the separate, although potentially related, question of karma. Here again, there is a mix of philosophy, religion and popular superstition associated with the concept of karma, essentially, "cause and effect". There remain questions about why good people suffer, or why some are born into circumstances that are filled with luxury and ease, while others have to struggle and suffer under terrible burdens. Buddhism has perhaps had the most to say on the law of karma, the chain of consequences, and there are clearly many things to be learned from their insights.

Rebirth and the law of karma have occupied humanity for many millennia all around the world. It is a subject that requires observation, reflection, insight and inner experience to come to any solid understanding.

In *Rebirth and Karma* Sri Aurobindo takes up these subjects in a systematic and comprehensive manner.

All page number citations in the following review are based on the U.S. edition of *Rebirth and Karma* published by Lotus Press, EAN: 978-0-9415-2463-6

The quotations cited in this book are by Sri Aurobindo from *Rebirth and Karma*. Each separate reading references the appropriate chapter upon which it is based or from which it was sourced, along with the pages. These citations are based on the US edition of *Rebirth and Karma* published by Lotus Press, Twin Lakes, WI. A few quotations from the *The Life Divine* came from the U.S. edition of *The Life Divine*, by Sri Aurobindo, published by Lotus Press.

Section I

Rebirth and Karma

Chapter One

Rebirth

Theories About Rebirth

There are numerous ideas, theories and concepts related to the question of whether or not we are reborn in some form or another after the death of the body. Some of these ideas hold that the life we live here is simply a single lifetime with nothing preceding it, and nothing following. Others hold that the life has no lives preceding it, and after death we are then transported to a paradise of heaven, or a punishment of hell, or some kind of limbo of purgatory. For some, the after death state is "permanent"; while for others it is an interregnum preparatory to a re-entry into the world.

Among the theories that believe in a recurrent series of births, there are also many viewpoints and a diverse terminology. Sri Aurobindo discusses some of these terms and the concepts behind them: "In former times the doctrine used to pass in Europe under the grotesque name of transmigration which brought with it to the Western mind the humorous image of the soul of Pythagoras migrating, a haphazard bird of passage, from the human form divine into the body of a guinea-pig or an ass."

Alternatively, "The philosophical appreciation of the theory expressed itself in the admirable but rather unmanageable Greek word, metempsychosis, which means the insouling of a new body by the same psychic individual."

"Reincarnation is the now popular term, but the idea in the word leans to the gross or external view of the fact and begs many questions."

Sri Aurobindo's own preference was to use the term "rebirth", "...for it renders the sense of the wide, colourless, but sufficient Sanskrit term, punarjanma, "again-birth," and commits us to nothing but the fundamental idea which is the essence and life of the doctrine."

Sri Aurobindo, *Rebirth and Karma*, Section I, Chapter 1, Rebirth, pg. 3

Can We Prove or Disprove Rebirth?

Sri Aurobindo discusses the question of rebirth, starting from the question of whether it can be proven or not; and by what methodology we need to evaluate it. "Rebirth is for the modern mind no more than a speculation and a theory; it has never been proved by the methods of modern science or to the satisfaction of the new critical mind formed by a scientific culture. Neither has it been disproved; for modern science knows nothing about a before-life or an after-life for the human soul, knows nothing indeed about a soul at all, nor can know; its province stops with the flesh and brain and nerve the embryo and its formation and development. Neither has modern criticism any apparatus by which the truth or untruth of rebirth can be established."

Sri Aurobindo points out that even questions such as the historicity of Christ remain an open-ended debate for the modern intellect. How then can subtle questions that go beyond the capacities of the physical senses and outside the framework of the physical world be evaluated?

The question of rebirth then becomes for most of us, simply a matter of argument or belief without any factual basis or support to underpin it. We argue one side or the other of the matter, but without any final certainty. "One argument, for instance, often put forward triumphantly in disproof is this that we have no memory of our past lives and therefore there were no past lives!" Sri Aurobindo describes the fallacy of this argument, in that most of us cannot remember our infancy or much of our childhood, but that does not make them any less real! "How much do we remember of our actual lives which we are undoubtedly living at the present moment? Our memory is normally good for what is near, becomes vaguer or less comprehensive as its objects recede into the distance, farther off seizes only some salient points and, finally, for the beginning of our lives falls into a mere blankness." Sri Aurobindo continues: "Yet we demand that this physical memory, this memory of the brute brain of man which cannot remember our infancy and has lost so much of our later years, shall recall that which was before infancy, before birth, before itself was formed. And if it cannot, we are to cry, "Disproved your reincarnation theory!"

Clearly we require instruments and capabilities beyond those of the physical mind and senses to experience and understand experiences that are not able to be perceived by the physical mind and senses. Similarly, the question of rebirth must then be researched and understood using different criteria and tools of understanding. Sri Aurobindo calls this a "psychical memory".

Sri Aurobindo, *Rebirth and Karma*, Section I, Chapter 1, Rebirth, pp. 3-5

Difficulties in Proving the Existence of Rebirth to the Scientific Mind

Sri Aurobindo points out that even if we were able to elicit various proofs of the memory of past lives, it remains difficult for the scientific mind to accept these proofs, since they would not be subject to the type of physical factual scrutiny which that mind finds as its sole basis for acceptance. On the contrary, even cases that would be considered extremely positive can be explained away by those who choose to do so through any number of doubts or issues that can cloud the results.

We have of course heard of the cases where an individual is born in one country, and as a very young child is able to describe a village halfway across the world in another country to a "T" without prior exposure to that village; and that further, the child was able to describe circumstances of a past life with specific individuals who were found to be historical individuals. Even in such clear cases, however, the physical mind, resistant to anything beyond its range of knowledge, finds arguments or objections.

Harder to explain are cases where an individual not only has such clear and factual knowledge, but can even speak in a different language to which that person has not been exposed in the current lifetime.

Such cases, since they have been documented, lend tremendous weight to the idea that rebirth must exist, at least for those who have not tried to limit themselves solely to the knowledge available to the 5 limited senses.

The doubters can devise any number of excuses. "It might be maintained that they prove the power of a certain mysterious faculty in us, a consciousness that can have some inexplicable knowledge of past events, but that these events may belong to other personalities than ours and that our attribution of them to our own personality in past lives is an imagination, a hallucination, or else an instance of that self-appropriation of things and experiences perceived but not our own which is one out of the undoubted phenomena of mental error."

While an abundance of such experiences and documentation would tend to lend weight and credence to the acceptance of rebirth, clearly it is not possible to prove things to the physical mind that it does not want to admit. There remain those today who will not recognise the fossil history of the earth and the time-frames that this history denotes; or even, that the earth is not the center of the universe!

Sri Aurobindo, *Rebirth and Karma*, Section I, Chapter 1, Rebirth, pp. 5-6

Proof, Moral Certitude and Reason

Before reviewing the theory of rebirth through the lens of our reasoning faculty, Sri Aurobindo first takes up the very question of the limitations of the reasoning faculty itself to establish the proof of anything. "After all, most of the things that we accept as truths are really no more than moral certitudes."

He goes on to illustrate that over time, we have propounded various explanations for the astronomical events we see, each one of which was accepted as the "truth" (to the point where it became punishable by torture and death to contradict that truth during the time of the Holy Inquisition), only to later give way to a new explanation that became the new "truth" for some period of time. The Newtonian universe has subsequently been superseded by the premises of quantum physics and today the concept of the truth of the universe is far different than it was just 100 years ago.

Sri Aurobindo discusses these issues: "This is the ever-perplexing and inherent plague of our reason; for it starts by knowing nothing and has to deal with infinite possibilities, and the possible explanations of any given set of facts until we actually know what is behind them, are endless. In the end, we really know only what we observe and even that subject to a haunting question, for instance, that green is green and white is white, although it appears that colour is not colour but something else that creates the appearance of colour. Beyond observable fact we must be content with reasonable logical satisfaction, dominating probability and moral certitude,–at least until we have the sense to observe that there are faculties in us higher than the sense-dependent reason and awaiting development by which we can arrive at greater certainties."

It is useful to explore the limitations of the reasoning faculty before we dive into the question of rebirth, because the very facts we need to review in regarding rebirth go beyond the realm of proof within the limits of the reason. We may be able to approach moral certitude, as we have done in other fields of review, but proof would have to await the action of higher and deeper faculties of knowledge.

Sri Aurobindo, *Rebirth and Karma*, Section I, Chapter 1, Rebirth, pg. 6

Occam's Razor and the Theory of Rebirth

Occam's razor, which essentially is the concept that when all other things are equal, the simplest explanation will tend to be the best, is a useful conceptual tool in many fields of life, and helps us avoid bogging down in needless complexity,–thereby helping us sort out theories that have "too many moving parts" to sustain serious scrutiny. This is especially helpful when it comes to practical matters in the material world, but it is not always the answer! Sri Aurobindo uses the example of the simple explanation of the "theory of the spheres" as an explanation of astronomical events. Today we have a much more detailed and complex understanding, as well as the ability to observe many more facts that need to be covered by any solution.

This becomes a question because the theory of rebirth and the corollary law of karma actually is a quite good example of "Occam's razor". Sri Aurobindo explains: "The theory of rebirth coupled with that of Karma gives us a simple, symmetrical, beautiful explanation of things..."

If we accepted Occam's razor as a determining factor, we would have to admit that *Rebirth and Karma* are the best explanation we have for the facts of our existence. Sri Aurobindo cautions however, that while this may provide us "moral certitude", it does not yet constitute certainty or absolute proof and thus, much more examination of the question is warranted.

Sri Aurobindo, *Rebirth and Karma*, Section I, Chapter 1, Rebirth, pp. 6-7

Heredity and Rebirth

Modern science recognizes that there are factors that help to predetermine the physical characteristics of the individual being. These factors carry forward through physical transmission from ancestors and help to determine the capacities and physical attributes of the being. This is called "heredity". Heredity primarily deals with physical characteristics and as a theory, it has done a good job in explaining many things. It has, however, not succeeded as well in terms of explaining issues such as personality, the phenomenon of genius or prodigy traits, or emotional character. Heredity is also not as "cut and dried" as many believe, inasmuch as different children born into the same family to the same parents can have totally different physical traits, as well as intellects.

There is of course also the debate about the influence of environment on the individual development, but that is not relevant to the current review. "Nature vs. Nurture" is of course an interesting subject that deserves its own scrutiny in its own place.

Turning to the question of rebirth, Sri Aurobindo explains that "Rebirth accounts, for example, for the phenomenon of genius, inborn faculty and so many other psychological mysteries."

No theory of heredity can explain the ability of Mozart or Beethoven as young children to create musical compositions and play them. Nor can it be explained away by training or "nurture". Once we get into the cases of talents and capacities that are far beyond the norm, outside the capacities of the parents and outside the specific training and focus the parents provide, it becomes even more obvious that there is something at work here beyond pure heredity or training.

This is one area where rebirth actually begins to illuminate the issue; but it does not stop there. *Rebirth and Karma* are able to provide solutions to other issues that are not explicable otherwise, as we shall see hereafter.

Sri Aurobindo, *Rebirth and Karma*, Section I, Chapter 1, Rebirth, pp. 7-8

The Ethical Argument for
Rebirth and Karma Does Not Stand Scrutiny

We see apparently good men who suffer and bad men who prosper. We find this unaccountable in a world in which a just God rules and we expect the good to get rewards and the bad to be punished. When this does not occur in this lifetime, some religions put it off to a "heaven" or a "hell" after death in which God's judgment about our lives is carried out upon us for eternity.

Even those who subscribe to *Rebirth and Karma* as the mechanism for a progression through lives tend to add on a type of ethical element to this to explain why it is that we see bad getting away with things apparently and the good facing inexplicable obstacles and suffering. It then gets explained away as a result of that particular "person" in a past life having done good or bad deeds which are now being rewarded or punished here; and similarly, the good or bad deeds in this lifetime will carry into future lives.

A deeper review of this however makes it clear that there is no such divine ledger being kept that automatically metes out exactly what each individual has "earned" in terms of rewards or punishments across multiple lifetimes. To truly begin to understand the concepts of *Rebirth and Karma* we need to first address these unfortunate accretions that have been formed around them.

Sri Aurobindo comments on this issue: "For it is intolerable that man with his divine capacity should continue to be virtuous for a reward and shun sin out of terror. Better a strong sinner than a selfish virtuous coward or a petty huckster with God; there is more divinity in him, more capacity of elevation."

"And it is inconceivable that the system of this vast and majestic world should have been founded on these petty and paltry motives."

Sri Aurobindo, *Rebirth and Karma*, Section I, Chapter 1, Rebirth, pp. 8-10

The True Foundation of the Theory of Rebirth

Sri Aurobindo has dismissed the concept of material reward and punishment as being the basis for action underlying *Rebirth and Karma*. He now provides the actual rationale under which *Rebirth and Karma* are not simply a theory among theories, but an essential mechanism to the operation of life and evolution.

"The true foundation of the theory of rebirth is the evolution of the soul, or rather its efflorescence out of the veil of Matter and its gradual self-finding."

"And if this gradual efflorescence be true, then the theory of rebirth is an intellectual necessity, a logically unavoidable corollary."

The reason it becomes necessary is based in the purpose of the soul's evolution. "Not conventional or interested virtue and the faultless counting out of the small coin of good in the hope of an apportioned material reward, but the continual growth towards a divine knowledge, strength, love and purity. These things alone are real virtue and this virtue is its own reward. The one true reward of the works of love is to grow ever in capacity and delight of love up to the ecstasy of the spirit's all-seizing embrace and universal passion; the one reward of the works of right Knowledge is to grow perpetually into the infinite Light; the one reward of the works of right Power is to harbour more and more of the Force Divine, and of the works of purity to be freed more and more from egoism into that immaculate wideness where all things are transformed and reconciled into divine equality. To seek other reward is to bind oneself to a foolishness and a childish ignorance; and to regard even these things as a reward is an unripeness and an imperfection."

The process of the soul's expression and growth out of Matter, through the various challenges of Life, the developments of Mind and beyond into the Supramental ranges of consciousness is something that is not done in a single lifetime, and it is this process that requires and determines the continual rebirth and which is propelled forward through the chain of cause and effect, karma. That does not imply that a specific egoistic personality is reborn continually; rather that the stream of energy continues and develops through the process of life and death.

Sri Aurobindo, *Rebirth and Karma*, Section I, Chapter 1, Rebirth, pg. 10

The True Role of Prosperity and Adversity in the Soul's Evolution

It is quite understandable that we want to treat prosperity and beneficial things as a reward, and adversity and suffering as a punishment; and it is true that we use this system in terms of training ourselves and our children in how to act in the world in an appropriate manner. Humans have developed numerous ethical and moral codes, as well as external laws and commandments which we take pleasure in enforcing on others, even in cases where we are not so scrupulous ourselves!

All of this is supposed to be part of a larger universal moral law of the Creator, or some universal action of karma, but in reality, it seems like these are constructs of the human mind, fueled by the vital nature's demand for satisfaction and enjoyment, and that they do not actually represent the way the universe operates. It seems to be a case of "making god in man's image" more than a case of understanding the functional processes of the soul's evolution in the universe.

Sri Aurobindo describes the role of these "rewards" and "punishments" in terms of the soul's evolutionary impetus: "These are experiences of the soul in its training, helps, props, means, disciplines, tests, ordeals,–and prosperity often a worse ordeal than suffering. Indeed, adversity, suffering may often be regarded rather as a reward to virtue than as a punishment for sin, since it turns out to be the greatest help and purifier of the soul struggling to unfold itself. To regard it merely as the stern award of a Judge, the anger of an irritated Ruler or even the mechanical recoil of result of evil upon cause of evil is to take the most superficial view possible of God's dealings with the soul and the law of the world's evolution."

Sri Aurobindo points out that even in worldly matters, we should look upon the goals and benefits differently: "And what of worldly prosperity, wealth, progeny, the outward enjoyment of art, beauty, power? Good, if they be achieved without loss to the soul and enjoyed only as the outflowing of the divine Joy and Grace upon our material existence. But let us seek them first for others or rather for all, and for ourselves only as a part of the universal condition or as one means of bringing perfection nearer."

Sri Aurobindo, *Rebirth and Karma*, Section I, Chapter 1, Rebirth, pp. 10-11

Consciously Immortal

So long as we try to understand the concept of rebirth using the faculties of the mind, it is impossible to come to any solid basis. Due to the limitations of the mind and its faculties of perception and understanding, we are left with conflicting ideas and contradictory points of view. It is essentially impossible for the mind to grasp anything that is outside its normal range of focus and action, and clearly the operation of a universal process of development using rebirth as a mechanism goes far beyond the normal scope of the mental power.

This is not to say that the theory of rebirth is beyond any understanding. There are other faculties with other powers of understanding. Sri Aurobindo points this out: "The soul needs no proof of its rebirth any more than it needs proof of its immortality. For there comes a time when it is consciously immortal, aware of itself in its eternal and immutable essence. Once that realisation is accomplished, all intellectual questionings for and against the immortality of the soul fall away like a vain clamour of ignorance around the self-evident and ever-present truth."

Sri Aurobindo goes further: "That is the true dynamic belief in immortality when it becomes to us not an intellectual dogma but a fact as evident as the physical fact of our breathing and as little in need of proof or argument. So also there comes a time when the soul becomes aware of itself in its eternal and mutable movement; it is then aware of the ages behind that constituted the present organisation of the movement, sees how this was prepared in an uninterrupted past, remembers something of the bygone soul-states, environments, particular forms of activity which built up its present constituents and knows to what it is moving by development in an uninterrupted future. This is the true dynamic belief in rebirth, and there too the play of the questioning intellect ceases; the soul's vision and the soul's memory are all."

With this basis it is then possible to take a longer and harder look at the mechanism of rebirth and karma and to understand with a greater depth of insight and subtlety the complexity of the functioning of this process.

Sri Aurobindo, *Rebirth and Karma*, Section I, Chapter 1, Rebirth, pp. 11-12

CHAPTER TWO

THE REINCARNATING SOUL

How Do We Determine: What Is the Reincarnating Soul?

In reviewing the concept of rebirth, we need to be able to look at facts, assemble data, and understand things in a logical and consistent manner. Most of us tend to take things on faith, and devote little time to deep consideration of the issues. This is particularly true for those who accept or deny the theory of rebirth. The acceptance or the denial are generally based on little serious consideration, but rather, on a packaged concept that we either accept more or less blindly, or deny on the same basis. Sri Aurobindo points out that this is actually a tendency of the mind, when we get to more complex or tougher subject areas, but it is one which we should consciously overcome to truly understand what rebirth is about.

Sri Aurobindo's critique of the common views of rebirth is as follows: "The soul is reborn in a new body,–that vague and almost meaningless assertion is for them sufficient. But what is the soul and what can possibly be meant by the rebirth of a soul? Well, it means reincarnation; the soul, whatever that may be, had got out of one case of flesh and is now getting into another case of flesh."

"But what is it that thus "leaves" one body and "enters" into another? Is it another, a psychic body and subtle form, that enters into the gross corporeal form,–the Purusha perhaps of the ancient image, no bigger than a man's thumb, or is it something in itself formless and impalpable that incarnates in the sense of becoming or assuming to the senses a palpable shape of bone and flesh?"

If we go just this far we do not gain any clear sense of the nature of the soul or the nature of the rebirth process. It warrants substantial further review and consideration.

Sri Aurobindo, *Rebirth and Karma*, Section I, Chapter 2, The Reincarnating Soul, pp. 13-14

The Common View About Reincarnation

As we go through life, we experience different stages, from childhood, through youth, adulthood and old age. There is to our internal sense an experience of continuity. We can reflect back through the preceding stages and recognize a consistent "person" that is experiencing these stages.

It is therefore quite natural for the first impression about rebirth to be based on the idea that this same "consistent person" moves from one life to another. Even among those who do not accept the idea of rebirth, but who believe in an eternal heaven or hell after death, the "person" experiencing these things is implied to be this "consistent person" we experience in a lifetime.

Sri Aurobindo describes it thus: "In the ordinary, the vulgar conception there is no birth of a soul at all, but only the birth of a new body into the world occupied by an old personality unchanged from that which once left some now discarded physical frame. It is John Robinson who has gone out of the form of flesh he once occupied; it is John Robinson who tomorrow or some centuries hence will re-incarnate in another form of flesh and resume the course of his terrestrial experiences with another name and in another environment."

It is more or less akin to changing a suit of clothes for another in the most common iteration of this idea.

Sri Aurobindo points out that this idea is especially appealing. "For it is the extinction or dissolution of the personality, of this mental, nervous and physical composite which I call myself that is hard to bear for the man enamoured of life, and it is the promise of its survival and physical reappearance that is the great lure."

The real problem, from the common viewpoint, is that we do not have any clear memory or sense of that continuity between birth and birth as we do within the framework of a single lifetime. We want to have the awareness of continuity and failing that we do not see the purpose or experience the positive enjoyment of the extended life of the "consistent person". People who take this view therefore in some cases try to establish a continuity through practices such as "past life regression" therapy. Others provide explanations for the lack of memory, such as that propounded in the Aeneid, whereby when a man dies, he goes to the underworld, and when the time comes for returning to earth, he first goes into the river of Lethe which removes all memory of the past life.

Clearly there are limitations to the idea that a single "consistent person" moves from life to life, even if we acknowledge and accept the

Sri Aurobindo, *Rebirth and Karma*, Section I, Chapter 2, The Reincarnating Soul, pg. 14

A Buddhist Perspective on Rebirth

Sri Aurobindo surveys some of the wisdom traditions with respect to the light they can shed on the question of rebirth. In doing so, he is not attempting to provide a comprehensive, in-depth review of the subtlety, nuances and range of discussion within these traditions, but to highlight some of the key concepts that stem from that teaching. He begins with a Buddhist view of the matter:

"There is, he said, no self, no person; there is simply a continuous stream of energy in action like the continuous flowing of a river or the continuous burning of a flame. It is this continuity which creates in the mind the false sense of identity. I am not now the same person that I was a year ago, not even the same person that I was a moment ago, any more than the water flowing past yonder ghaut is the same water that flowed past it a few seconds ago; it is the persistence of the flow in the same channel that preserves the false appearance of identity. Obviously, then, there is no soul that reincarnates, but only Karma that persists in flowing continuously down an apparently uninterrupted channel. It is Karma that incarnates; Karma creates the form of a constantly changing mentality and physical bodies that are, we may presume, the result of that changing composite of ideas and sensations which I call myself. The identical "I" is not, never was, never will be. Practically, so long as the error of personality persists, this does not make much difference and I can say in the language of ignorance that I am reborn in a new body; practically, I have to proceed on the basis of that error. But there is this important point gained that it is all an error and an error which can cease; the composite can be broken up for good without any fresh formation, the flame can be extinguished, the channel which called itself a river destroyed. And then there is non-being, there is cessation, there is the release of the error from itself."

Sri Aurobindo, *Rebirth and Karma*, Section I, Chapter 2, The Reincarnating Soul, pp. 14-15

A Vedantic Perspective on Rebirth

The Katha Upanishad is framed as a dialogue between a young seeker after the truth of what happens to the person after death, and the Lord of Death, Yama. This dialogue sets forth the perspective of the Vedantic approach.

Sri Aurobindo clarifies the Vedantic approach: "he admits an identical, a self, a persistent immutable reality,-but other than my personality, other than this composite which I call myself." Vedanta frames the question of the survival of the personality thus: "...even the gods debated this of old and it is not easy to know, for subtle is the law of it; something survives that appears to be the same person, that descends into hell, that ascends into heaven, that returns upon the earth with a new body, but is it really the same person that thus survives? Can we really say of the man "He still is," or must we not rather say "This *he* no longer is"?

When the Lord of Death responds to Nachiketas, "Yama too in his answer speaks not at all of the survival of death, and he only gives a verse or two to a bare description of that constant rebirth which all serious thinkers admitted as a universally acknowledged truth. What he speaks of is the Self, the real Man, the Lord of all these changing appearances; without the knowledge of that Self the survival of the personality is not immortal life but a constant passing from death to death; he only who goes beyond personality to the real Person becomes the Immortal. Till then a man seems indeed to be born again and again by the force of his knowledge and works, name succeeds to name, form gives place to form, but there is no immortality."

Clearly the Vedantic view acknowledges something which persists, but this is not something tied, as in the popular conception, to a specific personality-entity. Rather, there is a Self which puts on the various bodies and personalities, gains the essence of the experiences in each lifetime and uses these to mature and grow.

Sri Aurobindo, *Rebirth and Karma*, Section I, Chapter 2, The Reincarnating Soul, pp. 15-16

Comparing the Buddhist and Vedantic Views of Rebirth

Both the Buddhist and the Vedantic approach agree that the individual consistent personality is essentially impermanent and a temporary formation, and that therefore it is not something that survives and is "reborn". Sri Aurobindo describes the process: "There is a constant reforming of personality in new bodies, but this personality is a mutable creation of force at work streaming forward in Time and never for a moment the same, and the ego-sense that makes us cling to the life of the body and believe readily that it is the same idea and form, that it is John Robinson who is reborn as Sidi Hossain, is a creation of the mentality. Achilles was not reborn as Alexander, but the stream of force in its works which created the momentarily changing mind and body of Achilles flowed on and created the momentarily changing mind and body of Alexander."

Thus far, there is general accord between the two views. The Vedantic view diverges in terms of what it is that "survives" and whether there is something other than simply the movement of a stream of energy. "Still, said the ancient Vedanta, there is yet something beyond this force in action, Master of it, one who makes it create for him new names and forms, and that is the Self, the Purusha, the Man, the Real Person. The ego-sense is only its distorted image reflected in the flowing stream of embodied mentality."

Thus, for either approach, the individual egoistic personality is not essential real or immortal. The personality any of us experiences in this lifetime is a temporary structure built up by the ego-sense for a transitory need and is not intended to survive eternity. Nevertheless, for the Vedantic approach, there is something that creates, uses and exceeds each of these individual forms.

Sri Aurobindo, *Rebirth and Karma*, Section I, Chapter 2, The Reincarnating Soul, pg. 16

What Inhabits the Body At Birth, Resides In the Body During Life and Departs At Death?

In order to gain a true understanding of the process and meaning of rebirth, we first need to come to some understanding of what in fact is being reborn. If it is not, as we have been reviewing, the individual personality that survives from life to life, then what is it?

Sri Aurobindo discusses this issue: "Is it then the Self that incarnates and reincarnates? But the Self is imperishable, immutable, unborn, undying. The Self is not born and does not exist in the body; rather the body is born and exists in the Self. For the Self is one everywhere,– in all bodies, we say, but really it is not confined and parceled out in different bodies except as the all-constituting ether seems to be formed into different objects and is in a sense in them."

Because we tend to evaluate things from the standpoint of our individual body and personal awareness, we actually confuse the facts of what is occurring. This is similar to our confusion about the sun rising and setting with the earth as the center, when, in fact, we now recognize this to be an erroneous interpretation of what is actually taking place. When we look at the process of birth and death, we describe it as the soul "inhabiting" the body or the soul "departing" from the body. But it is more correct to refer to this process as the Soul taking on a bodily form, and the Soul casting off the bodily form.

When we are born, some form of awareness enters into and enlivens the body. When we die, this awareness departs. This awareness creates a sense of individuality, the personality, the ego-sense, but even in the vital levels of the plant and animal we still see something that "animates" the physical matter and which is absent when that physical shell dies or dissolves. Sri Aurobindo provides us an answer to this question, while pointing out that this does not solve the larger question as of yet: "It is the subtle or psychical frame which is tied to the physical by the heart-strings, by the cords of life-force, of nervous energy which have been woven into every physical fibre."

Clearly there must be some over-arching consciousness which creates these mutable forms of personality. The solution must still be sought if we are going to truly understand the reality of the process and its significance.

Sri Aurobindo, *Rebirth and Karma*, Section I, Chapter 2, The Reincarnating Soul, pp. 16-17

The Mental Being Leader of the Life and Body

Since the Self is considered to be immutable, and outside the changes of Nature, we actually have two questions to resolve here. If the Self is not subject to change, it obviously cannot itself become subject to time, space and circumstance, i.e. the processes of rebirth and karma, birth, life and death. The Self stands outside of this process. The question then arises, what is it that actually becomes subjected to the process of rebirth and karma, and how does it differ from the immutable Self on one side, and the individual ego-personality on the other.

Sri Aurobindo discusses these questions: "We have in fact an immutable Self, a real Person, lord of this ever-changing personality which, again, assumes every-changing bodies, but the real Self knows itself always as above the mutation, watches and enjoys it, but is not involved in it. Through what does it enjoy the changes and feel them to be its own, even while knowing itself to be unaffected by them? The mind and ego-sense are only inferior instruments; there must be some more essential form of itself which the Real Man puts forth, puts in front of itself, as it were, and at the back of the changings to support and mirror them without being actually changed by them. This more essential form is or seems to be in man the mental being or mental person which the Upanishads speak of as the mental leader of the life and body, *manomayah prana-sarira-neta*. It is that which maintains the ego-sense as a function in the mind and enables us to have the firm conception of continuous identity in Time as opposed to the timeless identity of the Self."

Sri Aurobindo, *Rebirth and Karma*, Section I, Chapter 2, The Reincarnating Soul, pg. 17

The Nature of the Changing Temporal Personality

The distinction between the Purusha, the unchanging witness consciousness, and Prakriti, the mutable nature, is useful to help us distinguish the complex interactions between the mental being, which has its basis in the Purusha, and the ego-personality that goes through changes of time, space and circumstance, and which is based in the Prakriti. This ego-personality is in fact made up of a number of different parts or layers that interact with each other and may in fact not always agree with one another in terms of the focus or direction.

With this basis of understanding, we can then look at the process of the mental being forming and developing a specific combination to create a new ego-personality in a new birth. Sri Aurobindo describes this process: "The mental being in resuming bodily life forms a new personality for its new terrestrial existence; it takes material from the common matter-stuff, life-stuff, mind-stuff of the physical world and during earthly life it is constantly absorbing fresh material, throwing out what is used up, changing its bodily, nervous and mental tissues. But this is all surface work; behind is the foundation of past experience held back from the physical memory so that the superficial consciousness may not be troubled or interfered with by the conscious burden of the past but may concentrate on the work immediately in hand. Still that foundation of past experience is the bed-rock of personality; and it is more than that. It is our real fund on which we can always draw even apart from our present superficial commerce with our surroundings. That commerce adds to our gains, modifies the foundation for a subsequent existence."

There is of course much more behind this surface interaction and ego-personality. This adds further layers of complexity that must be reviewed and understood to get a more complete picture of what is really taking place when we speak of "rebirth" and "karma".

Sri Aurobindo, *Rebirth and Karma*, Section I, Chapter 2, The Reincarnating Soul, pp. 17-18

The Wider Context of the Process of Rebirth

The surface personality is a limited formation that represents only a small fraction of the actual reality of our existence. Western psychologists, led by C.G. Jung, have opened up the realm of the Collective Unconscious and shown how our personality is to some degree shaped and developed based on archetypal formations in this collective reservoir of imagery and psychical history. Sri Aurobindo has added to this the understanding that there are not only subconscious realms, but also super-conscious realms, and these super-conscious realms are also essential reservoirs for the surface personality and its formation.

"It is only a small part of ourselves which lives and acts in the energies of our earthly existence. As behind the physical universe there are worlds of which ours is only a last result, so also within us there are worlds of our self-existence which throw out this external form of our being. The subconscient, the super-conscient are oceans from which and to which this river flows."

Given the complexity of these various "layers" of existence and their impact and inter-relationship upon one another, it is not really accurate to speak about a specific soul being reborn. Sri Aurobindo's commentary on this point: "There is not a definite psychic entity getting into a new case of flesh; there is a metempsychosis, a reinsouling, a rebirth of new psychic personality as well as a birth of a new body. And behind is the Person, the unchanging entity, the Master who manipulates this complex material, the Artificer of this wonderful artifice."

In conclusion: "to view ourselves as such and such a personality getting into a new case of flesh is to stumble about in the ignorance, to confirm the error of the material mind and the senses. The body is a convenience, the personality is a constant formation for whose development action and experience are the instruments; but the Self by whose will and for whose delight all this is, is other than the body, other than the action and experience, other than the personality which they develop. To ignore it is to ignore the whole secret of our being."

Sri Aurobindo, *Rebirth and Karma*, Section I, Chapter 2, The Reincarnating Soul, pp. 18-19

CHAPTER THREE

REBIRTH, EVOLUTION, HEREDITY

Science Investigates Evolution and Heredity

The surface mentality of man begins with the physical world in his investigations. The processes at work in the physical world have been opening up their secrets to the unrelenting review of the scientific mind. Over the past 150+ years, the concepts of evolution, first enunciated by Charles Darwin in a systematic way, and heredity, have been both put forth and developed. The science of genetics has taken this to a greater precision of detail and we can now see and trace much of the physical development that has taken place during the course of evolution.

What is missing from this analysis, however, is any understanding of processes that are outside the purely physical realm, or that may be causative of things we see in the physical world. Unfortunately, the open-minded scientific investigator had put on blinders that only have allowed, for the most part, this spirit of open inquiry to permeate research on the physical plane. Sri Aurobindo discusses this issue: Science…"is determined… to explain every supra-physical phenomenon by some physical fact; psychological process of mind must not exist except as result or rendering of physiological process of body. This set resolution, apparently rational and cautious of ascertainable and firmly tangible truth, but really heroic in its paradoxical temerity, shuts up her chance of rapid discovery, for the present at least, in a fairly narrow circle. It taints too her extensions of physical truth into the psychological field with a pursuing sense of inadequacy. And this inadequacy in extended application is very evident in her theories of heredity and evolution when she forces them beyond their safe ground of physical truth and labours to illumine by them the subtle, complex, elusive phenomena of our psychological being."

As this research has, however, gone deeper into the issues of consciousness, particularly in the work of researchers such as

Jung or the developments in the field of quantum mechanics and even more esoteric views of the universe, it has started to become clear that while evolution and heredity can do a more than adequate job of describing the processes at work in life and physical bodies in the physical world, they do not explain causes, or the consciousness that creates and develops through use of these processes. Some modern scientists have even gone so far as to recognize that matter consists of energy, and that energy consists of consciousness. We reach thereby a frontier where we need to leave physical processes behind and enter the realms of the supra-physical, the realms of consciousness, the realms of the Spirit.

Sri Aurobindo, *Rebirth and Karma*, Section I, Chapter 3, Rebirth, Evolution, Heredity, pp. 20-21

An Evolutionary Creation

Scientists have spent the last 150 years observing, defining and refining the theory of evolution. As a result of their efforts, they have developed intensively the science of genetics including an understanding of the mechanism of heredity on the physical plane. While we can certainly expect that, as with all scientific advancement, there will certainly come about opportunities to discard portions of the theory, as well as modify and enhance other portions, we have seen the basic concept stand up to a tremendous amount of factual review and observation.

There remain those who, by simply denying the factual record of observation, who insist that evolution and heredity have no basis and that the entire universe was created in a matter of days by an external creator who dropped all beings "ready-made" into place.

There are those who take this viewpoint to the literal extreme, and others who look at it symbolically. The symbolic viewpoint opens up a pathway for an evolutionary process to occur in the material world, bringing about the possibility of understanding between the "creationist" and the "evolutionist" views of the world.

Sri Aurobindo discusses the issue: "One thing at least seems now intellectually certain, we can no longer believe that these suns and systems were hurled full-shaped and eternally arranged into boundless space and all these numberless species of being planted on earth ready-made and nicely tailored in several days or any number of days in a sudden outburst of caprice or Dionysiac excitement or crowded activity of mechanical conception by the fiat of a timeless Creator. The successive development which was summarily proposed by the ancient Hindu thinkers, the lower forms of being first, man afterwards as the crown of the Spirit's development of life on earth, has been confirmed by the patient and detailed scrutiny of physical science,–an aeonic development, though the farther Hindu conception of a constant repetition of the principle in cycles is necessarily incapable of physical evidence."

Sri Aurobindo, *Rebirth and Karma*, Section I, Chapter 3, Rebirth, Evolution, Heredity, pp. 21-22

Oneness and Diversity
in the Process of Creation

Western science presents us with the idea that the entire universe was created out of One original source in what is called the "big bang". From that point forward, we see the systematic development of galaxies, solar systems, suns and planets. Drilling down to the earth, we find a systematic development from the raw elements of physical nature, to the development of life in a diverse and ever-expanding assortment of life-forms and combinations.

Sri Aurobindo correlates the Upanishadic vision to this issue: "One thing more seems now equally certain that not only the seed of all life was one,–again the great intuition of the Upanishads foreruns the conclusions of the physical enquiry, one seed which the universal self-existence by process of force has disposed in many ways, *ekam bijam bahudha sakti-yogat,*–but even the principle of development is one and the structural groundplan too as it develops step by step, in spite of all departures to this side or that in the workings of the creative Force or the creative Idea."

Sri Aurobindo points out that while starting from one uniform starting point, Nature's process appears to be one that leads to virtually infinite variety as small modifications within a type create enormous diversity. "It almost looks as if in the process of her physical harmonies there was meant to be some formal effect or symbolic reproduction of the truth that all things are originally one being, but a one who insists on his own infinite diversity, and even a suggestion that there is in this eternal unity an eternal pluralism, the Infinite Being self-repeated in an infinite multiplicity of beings each unique and yet each the One."

Sri Aurobindo, *Rebirth and Karma*, Section I, Chapter 3, Rebirth, Evolution, Heredity, pg. 22

Observing and Understanding the Tree of Life

Sri Aurobindo begins the discussion of the evolutionary process in the physical universe with a description of what we observe: "...one plasmic seed, one developing ground-plan, an opulent number of varieties whose logical process would be by an ascending order which passes up through fine but still very distinct gradations from the crude to the complex, from the less organised to the more organised, from the inferior to the superior type."

This of course raises questions about the origin and development of this process, which Sri Aurobindo poetically calls the "tree of life". There are arguments made for a strict physical evolution with step-wise and incremental development; while there are also arguments for some kind of external creative Being or Force which has developed all these myriad forms out of some complex plan, has then put them forth in some pre-determined order and discontinued any further physical world development that we can see, having apparently created sufficient diversity of forms to be satisfied.....

Science has adopted the physical evolutionary side of this argument, and bases its conclusions on an enormous amount of factual evidence, fossil records and DNA tracking. There still remain gaps or what are called "missing links" but in general the progression holds together well and there is a logic and consistency to the pattern we see.

It may be that these "missing links" are simply "missing" although they may have existed at some point in time; or that they may still be located as research continues. Alternatively, there may be other factors involved to account for the development and evolution of consciousness which leads to a modification to the purely physical progression.

This approach clearly appears to have validity for the physical evolution, but it does not quite explain the development of humanity, and the development of consciousness or self-awareness. These issues speak to another process that "uses" but is not limited by the mechanism of the development in the physical plane. This may involve a type of advance that is not strictly a linear progression of physical forms, but rather, a development of a new type of physical form capable of manifesting consciousness of a higher order that is the actual driver of the process. The development of man and the higher mental and spiritual orders of the power of consciousness could be an indicator of this type of "leap" from one level to another with a corresponding advancement in the physical form.

Sri Aurobindo, *Rebirth and Karma*, Section I, Chapter 3, Rebirth, Evolution, Heredity, pp. 22-23

A Hidden Soul Process
Behind the Physical Evolution

When we observe the processes of physical nature, we see that there is a clear transmission of basic traits of existence from one generation to the next with a coherent and repeatable result. The oak tree creates a seed which in turn creates a new oak tree. We see beings of one species giving birth to beings of the same species. There is also an obvious hereditary pattern at a finer level of detail, which is detailed by scientists in the science of genetics. Specific physical traits are clearly capable of being passed on from one generation to the next. It is not as simple as direct transmission as the process actually is built to create variation and diversity, through mingling of genetic characteristics of the parents in the offspring, and through the process of recessive traits being passed along through this mingling process.

While there is also a certain amount of mutation in the genetic process, this is still within the genus/species and does not create new beings from old forms.

What is not covered effectively by these facts are the higher mental and spiritual capabilities which clearly cannot be explained by a purely physical genetic process. If all these capacities were strictly limited to physical genetic transmission, we would see a strict class heredity of capabilities. We would however be unable to account for some of the dramatic "anomalies" that occur all too frequently, and which show a mental and spiritual capacity not in evidence in the parental stock.

Sri Aurobindo addresses these questions: "We are called upon to admit that the human seed for instance, which does not contain a developed human consciousness, yet carries with it the powers of such a consciousness so that they reproduce themselves automatically in the thinking and organised mentality of the offspring. This, even if we have to accept it, is an inexplicable paradox unless we suppose either that there is something more behind, a psychical power behind the veil of material process, or else that mind is only a process of life and life only a process of matter. Therefore finally we have to suppose the physical theory capable of explaining by purely material causes and a material constitution the mystery of the emergence of life in matter and the equal mystery of the emergence of mind in life. It is here that difficulties begin to crowd in which convict it, so far at least, of a hopeless inadequacy, and the nature of that inadequacy, its crux, its stumbling-point leave room for just that something behind, something psychical, a hidden soul process and for a more complex and less materialistic account of the truth of evolution."

Sri Aurobindo, *Rebirth and Karma*, Section I, Chapter 3, Rebirth, Evolution, Heredity, pp. 23-24

Is Life Purely a Condition of Material Energy?

In the West there has been an ongoing debate between science and religion about the origin and development of life. This has led to a polarized viewpoint in which neither side has, for the most part, been able to see any common ground. The extreme of the scientific dogma in this regard holds that all phenomena of life and mind, all stirrings of consciousness, are purely a result of physical, material energy, and therefore, there is no "higher purpose" and given the right opportunity, life can be created through the provision of the proper elements and basic "requirements".

Sri Aurobindo makes the point that this scientific viewpoint can never actually be proven. He acknowledges that the powers of consciousness that manifest Life and Mind (and further developments) may rely on the appropriate framework and organisation of elements of the material energy in order to manifest and act, but that does not mean that they are CAUSED by these material elements.

"Even with regard to life, which is by a great deal the lesser difficulty, the discovery of certain chemical or other physical and mechanical conditions under which life can be stimulated to appear, will prove no more than that these are the favourable or necessary conditions for the manifestation of life in body,–such conditions there must be in the nature of things,–but not that life is not another new and higher power of the force of universal being. The connection of life responses with physical conditions and stimuli proves very clearly that life and matter are connected and that, as indeed they must do to coexist, the two kinds of energy act on each other,–a very ancient knowledge; but it does not get rid of the fact that the physical response is accompanied by an element which seems to be of the nature of a nervous excitement and an incipient or suppressed consciousness and is not the same thing as the companion physical reaction."

Sri Aurobindo, *Rebirth and Karma*, Section I, Chapter 3, Rebirth, Evolution, Heredity, pp. 24-25

Is Mind Purely a Condition of Material Energy?

The scientists who try to explain life by physical energy also try to explain mind the same way. Somehow a combination of chemicals and electrical impulses created the sonnets of Shakespeare or the higher mathematics of Albert Einstein! Sri Aurobindo takes strong exception to this viewpoint:

"…but no amount of correspondence can show how a physical response can be converted into or amount to or by itself constitute in result a conscious operation, a perception, emotion, thought-concept, or prove that love is a chemical product or that Plato's theory of ideas or Homer's Iliad or the cosmic consciousness of the Yogin was only a combination of physiological reactions or a complex of the changes of grey brain matter or a flaming marvel of electrical discharges. It is not only that common sense and imagination boggle at these theories,–that objection may be disregarded,–not only that perception, reason and intuition have to be thrust aside in favour of a forced and too extended inference, but that there is a gulf of difference here between the thing to be explained and the thing by which it is sought to explain it which cannot be filled up, however much we may admit the nervous connections and psycho-physical bridges."

From a purely logical standpoint, nothing can develop that is not already inherent or involved in the starting point. So, for life and mind to manifest out of physical matter, material energy, they must already be involved therein. When we look closely at Matter, we see that it in fact is made up of highly organized and extremely powerful Energy. Even modern scientists have begun to recognize that Energy is not the ultimate term, but that Energy consists of Consciousness. Since Matter itself is not the starting point, it cannot be the first cause of life and mind! Clearly we are moving toward an understanding that Consciousness is the cause and Matter is the effect, and thus, as Life and Mind begin to manifest out of Matter, they are expressions of Consciousness.

The real work, the real review, therefore must take place at the level of Consciousness, if we are to understand the real nature of our existence.

Sri Aurobindo, *Rebirth and Karma*, Section I, Chapter 3, Rebirth, Evolution, Heredity, pp. 25-26

Soul Evolution and Physical Evolution, Heredity and Rebirth

Western scientists, starting from the physical world and material energy, eventually reach a point where they cannot go any further in terms of explaining the appearance, development and significance of life and consciousness. As they push against the boundaries of Matter, they are discovering worlds of ordered energy and consciousness.

the ancient Vedic seers and sages concluded long ago that Matter is a subordinate term and that it is the result, not the cause of what is manifesting and evolving. The idea of a soul evolution, utilizing the framework of the Material world and ordered processes of heredity, physical evolution and rebirth, arose from the insights of these sages, and it has the benefit of actually fitting the observable conditions better than the results obtained by the physical scientists of the modern world.

Sri Aurobindo explains: "Here too there is the evolutionary idea, but physical and life evolution, even the growth of mind, are held to be only incidental to a soul evolution of which Time is the course and the earth among many other worlds the theatre. In the old Indian version of this theory evolution, heredity and rebirth are three companion processes of the universal unfolding, evolution the processional aim, rebirth the main method, heredity one of the physical conditions. That is a theory which provides at least the framework for a harmonious explanation of all the complex elements of the problem. The scientific idea starts from the physical being and makes the psychical a result and circumstance of the body; this other evolutionary idea starts from soul and sees in the physical being an instrumentation for the awakening to itself of a spirit absorbed in the universe of Matter."

Sri Aurobindo, *Rebirth and Karma*, Section I, Chapter 3, Rebirth, Evolution, Heredity, pg. 26

Chapter Four

Rebirth and Soul Evolution

Limitations of the Reason to the Process of Knowledge

Inasmuch as the question of rebirth is not easily viewed from the surface of our lives, we need to involve the faculty of Reason to come to an understanding of this issue. We then are faced with understanding the limitations that the Reason has in terms of its ability to observe and understand what it is observing. Sri Aurobindo separates two types of Reason, the practical intelligence that is concerned primarily with results in the world, and the more abstract reasoning intelligence that attempts to understand principles, concepts and significances.

The practical Reason is essentially incapable of attaining a deeper understanding as it is willing to accept anything that allows it to succeed at its immediate task or focus. Sri Aurobindo points out that "Whether it corresponds to or is directly in touch with any real reality of things seems to be very much a matter of accident. It seems to be sufficient if we can persuade our facile and complaisant reason of its truth and find it serviceable and fruitful in consequences for thought, action and life-experience."

The second type of Reason does seek after greater things and tries to look behind the surface appearances, but it is limited by its connection to the practical intelligence as well. "But the workings of this calmer greater reason are hampered by two tremendous difficulties. First, it seems next to impossible to disengage it entirely from the rest of ourselves, from the normal intellectuality, from the will to believe, from that instinct of the intelligence which helps the survival, by a sort of subtle principle of preference and selection, of the way of thinking that suits our personal bent or the accomplished frame of our nature. And again, what is the Truth that our reason mirrors? It is after all some indirect image of Truth, not her very self and body seen face to face; it is an image moulded from such data, symbol, process of Reality,–if any real Reality there is,–as we can gather from the very limited experience of self and existing things open to the human mind."

The human mind is not actually suited, nor capable of directly knowing and apprehending Reality. It takes other and greater faculties to move beyond the mind's limitations. So when we rely on the mind, we are left with both our pre-determined self-selection of facts and ideas that favor our practical and ideational bent, and with a faculty that itself has strict limits to its powers.

Sri Aurobindo, *Rebirth and Karma*, Section I, Chapter 4, Rebirth and Soul Evolution, pg. 27

The Reason Attempts to Understand the Meaning Of Our Existence

Sri Aurobindo describes the issues surrounding the limitation of the Reason when it comes to the ultimate questions of life: "Nowhere are these disabilities more embarrassing than in those fundamental questions of the nature of the world and of our own existence which yet most passionately interest thinking humanity because this is in the end the thing of utmost importance to us, since everything else, except some rough immediate practicality of the moment, depends on its solution. And even that, until this great question is settled, is only a stumbling forward upon a journey of which we know not the goal or the purpose, the meaning or the necessity."

Religion, philosophy and science all attempt to provide solutions to these questions. Despite each one's claims to have a monopoly on the ultimate truth of their viewpoint, they all suffer from the self-filtering bias and from the overall limitations of the faculty of Reason and thus, they too fail to provide any final and definitive answers, as evidenced by the numerous different answers provided by them throughout mankind's history.

Whether based on speculation, reason, or some type of revealed experience, we find the same type of limitations in science, philosophy and religion. The underlying problem is the inability of the faculty of Reason to encompass and comprehend the complexity and enormity of the universal creation. The method of "knowing" makes it impossible to provide a comprehensive answer from this standpoint.

Sri Aurobindo briefly recounts the issues for each of these paths: "The religions profess to solve these grand problems with an inspired or revealed certainty; but the enormity of their differences shows that in them too there is a selection of ideas, separate aspects of the Truth...and a construction from a limited spiritual experience." "The philosophical systems are very obviously only feasible selective constructions of great reflective ideas. More often these are possibilities of the reason much rather than assured certainties or, if founded on spiritual experience, they are still selective constructions, a sort of great architectural approach to some gate into unknowable Divine or ineffable Infinite." "The system of science seems to be itself only another feasible and fruitful construction of the reason giving a

serviceable account to itself of the physical world and our relations to it, and it seems to be nothing more. And its knowledge
is fatally bound by the limitation of its data and its outlook."

Sri Aurobindo, *Rebirth and Karma*, Section I, Chapter 4, Rebirth and Soul Evolution, pg. 28

Three Characteristic Stances of the Mind of Reason

Sri Aurobindo continues his exploration of the human reason as a preliminary to the review of the issues surrounding the concept of rebirth. It is essential to understand the powers and limitations of the reason depending on the starting point of the individual exercising this power, so that we can understand the rationale that leads to reactions or responses and adjust for them. Sri Aurobindo describes the characteristic stance of the religious, philosophical and skeptical minds.

"...the religious mind accepts the theory or assumption...with faith, with a will of belief, with an emotional certainty, and finds its verification in an increasing spiritual intuition and experience."

"The philosophic mind accepts it calmly and discerningly for its coherent agreement with the facts and necessities of being; it verifies by a pervading and unfailing harmony with all the demands of reason and intellectualised intuition."

"But the sceptical mind–not the mind of mere doubt or dogmatic denial which usually arrogates that name, but the open and balanced mind of careful, impartial and reserved inquiry,–gives a certain provisional character to its hypotheses, and it verifies by the justification of whatever order or category of ascertainable facts it takes for its standard of proof and invests with a character of decisive authority or reality."

Sri Aurobindo not only recognizes the validity in its own type of each of these three, but he points out that ideally we should be able to utilize all three in our review of facts and questions, in order to optimize the potential result. "For if the sceptical or provisional attitude makes us more ready to modify our image of Truth in the light of new material of thought and knowledge, the religious mind also, provided it keeps a certain firm and profound openness to new spiritual experience, can proceed faster to a larger and larger light, and meanwhile we can walk by it with an assured step and go securely about our principal business of the growth and perfection of our being. The philosophic mind has the use of giving a needed largeness and openness to our mentality,–if it too does not narrow itself by a close circle of metaphysical dogma,–and supports besides the harmony of our other action by the orderly assent of the higher reason."

Sri Aurobindo, *Rebirth and Karma*, Section I, Chapter 4, Rebirth and Soul Evolution, pp. 28-29

Soul Realities and Soul Process

The Reason, in its clearest and widest operation, while unable to grasp ultimate Reality and ultimate Truth, is able to at least provide a framework for understanding of process in the physical world.

Sri Aurobindo points out that "For if there is one thing now certain it is that physical science may give clues of process, but cannot lay hold on the reality of things. That means that the physical is not the whole secret of world and existence, and that in ourselves too the body is not the whole of our being. It is then through something supraphysical in Nature and ourselves which we may call the soul, whatever the exact substance of soul may be, that we are likely to get that greater truth and subtler experience which will enlarge the narrow rigid circle traced by physical science and bring us nearer to the Reality."

When we admit that there are supraphysical realities to the universe that cannot be directly or completely comprehended by the action of Reason, we can open to the possibilities offered by other forms of experience, for instance, spiritual experience. These experiences have an overwhelming and vivid impact on those who receive them, and they are the foundational experiences behind virtually all of the major religions throughout the world. Sri Aurobindo points out "...there is nothing to prevent us from proceeding firmly upon whatever certitudes of spiritual experience have become to us the soil of our inner growth or the pillars on our road to self-knowledge. These are soul realities. But the exact frame we shall give to that knowledge, will best be built by farther spiritual experience aided by new enlarged intuitions, confirmed in the suggestions of a wide philosophic reason and fruitfully using whatever helpful facts we may get from the physical and the psychic sciences. These are truths of soul process; their full light must come by experimental knowledge and observation of the world without us and the world within."

Sri Aurobindo, *Rebirth and Karma*, Section I, Chapter 4, Rebirth and Soul Evolution, pp. 29-30

The Individual Soul and the Theory of Rebirth

If the physical world is the cause and mechanism of existence, with no further significance or higher development, the question of rebirth is unnecessary. Similarly, if there is an "all-soul" that develops without regard to the individual development specifically, rebirth is also unnecessary. In order to have a significance to the concept of rebirth, there must be some type of individual soul that evolves and develops, and thereby needs and utilizes the process of rebirth. The existence of an individual soul does not imply that rebirth actually takes place as there are other possible explanations, but without an individual soul, there is no sense in a process involving rebirth.

Sri Aurobindo addresses these questions: "Now the question of rebirth turns almost entirely upon the one fundamental question of the past of the individual being and its future. If the creation of the whole nature is to be credited to the physical birth, then the body, life and soul of the individual are only a continuation of the body, life and soul of his ancestry, and there is no room anywhere for soul rebirth. The individual man has no past being independent of them and can have no independent future; he can prolong himself in his progeny…but there is no other rebirth for him. No continued stream of individuality presided over by any mental or spiritual person victoriously survives the dissolution of the body. On the other hand, if there is any element in us, still more the most important of all, which cannot be so accounted for, but presupposes a past or admits a future evolution other than that of the race mind and the physical ancestry, then some kind of soul birth becomes a logical necessity."

Sri Aurobindo, *Rebirth and Karma*, Section I, Chapter 4, Rebirth and Soul Evolution, pp. 30-31

Individual Soul or Universal Soul

The question of whether there is an individual soul that can grow, develop and evolve, or whether there is a universal soul of which each individual is simply a "data-point" is the next issue to be resolved before looking at the question of rebirth. Rebirth has no essential meaning if there is no individual soul to benefit from it.

If we overview the development of the physical and vital life, we can see the role of a process which scientists have identified as evolution. The physical characteristics are carried forward by the process called heredity and there has been established a well-developed framework for understanding this physical evolution. This does not preclude the action of some other motivating factor that uses the process, of course.

Where the processes of physical evolution seem not to be able to explain things as well is in the development of the higher mental, and spiritual, processes and capabilities. There is in fact a debate in the West about the varying impact of "nature" versus "nurture" (heredity vs. environment) as a shaping factor in the development of the individual personality and its characteristics including the higher mental, emotional and psychical responses.

This brings us then to the question Sri Aurobindo addresses at this point. The combination of the physical heredity with the environmental influences and pressures could represent the development of a "universal soul" as the central premise of existence. "…we may say that they are a phase of the universal soul, a part of the process of its evolution by selection; the race, not the individual, is the continuous factor and all our individual effort and acquisition, only in appearance, not really independent, ceases with death, except so much of our gain as is chosen to be carried on in the race by some secret will or conscious necessity in the universal being or the persistent becoming."

If this is the ultimate truth of our existence, then, of course, there is no necessity of rebirth, as the forward development momentum is taking place in the universal being and each individual life is simply a cog or grain in a larger mechanism or existence.

Sri Aurobindo, *Rebirth and Karma*, Section I, Chapter 4, Rebirth and Soul Evolution, pg. 31

The Existence of the Individual Soul Evolving Through Time Establishes Rebirth

When we begin to experience the higher spiritual parts of our nature, we recognize that here there is something which is clearly beyond the physical material manifestation and independent from it. We thus have found the basis for accepting conclusively the need for and the reality of rebirth. Our spiritual nature can adopt a standpoint which is able to observe and either give consent, or withhold consent, to the actions of the mind, life and body. This portion of our being, which we may designate the "soul", is not limited by physical heredity or by the influence of environmental factors. We can observe, and even participate in, the evolutionary development of the soul.

Sri Aurobindo points out: "Quite apart from any evidence of an after life on other planes or any memory of past births, this is sufficient warrant for a refusal to accept as sufficient any theory of the ephemeral being of the individual and the sole truth of the evolutionary Universal. Certainly, the individual being is not thereby shown to be independent of the All-Soul; it may be nothing but a form of it in time. But it is sufficient for our purpose that it is a persistent soul form, not determined by the life of the body and ceasing with its dissolution, but persisting independently beyond. For if it is thus independent of the physical race continuity in the future, if it thus shows itself capable of determining its own future soul evolution in time, it must have had secretly such an independent existence all through and it must have been determining in reality, though no doubt by some other and indirect insistence, its past soul evolution too in time."

It is possible that the individual soul is either a portion of the All-Soul, or independent of it. Either way, as long as there IS an independent individual soul that evolves through time, the process of rebirth becomes a given. "But it is sufficient for the theory of rebirth that a secret soul continuity of the individual does exist and not alone a brute succession of bodies informed by the All-Soul with a quite ephemeral illusion of mental or spiritual individuality."

Sri Aurobindo, *Rebirth and Karma*, Section I, Chapter 4, Rebirth and Soul Evolution, pg. 32

A Future Without a Past?

One widespread notion about the soul is that it is created with the birth in this lifetime, but then exists eternally into the future. In this view, there is no precedent for the circumstances into which we are placed, and it is nevertheless our responsibility to deal with these circumstances and make the best of them for the benefit of our (future) eternal existence (however that is envisioned).

The idea of an eternal future without a past is a logical inconsistency. Sri Aurobindo describes the issue as follows: "It involves the difficulty of a creature beginning in time but enduring through all eternity, an immortal being dependent for its existence on an act of physical generation, yet itself always and entirely unphysical and independent of the body which results from the generation. These are objections insuperable to the reason. But there is too the difficulty that this soul inherits a past for which it is in no way responsible, or is burdened with mastering propensities imposed on it not by its own act, and is yet responsible for its future which is treated as if it were in no way determined by that often deplorable inheritance....or that unfair creation, and were entirely of its own making. We are made helplessly what we are and are yet responsible for what we are,–or at least for what we shall be hereafter, which is inevitably determined to a large extent by what we are originally. And we have only this one chance. Plato and the Hottentot, the fortunate child of saints or Rishis and the born and trained criminal plunged from beginning to end in the lowest fetid corruption of a great modern city have equally to create by the action or belief of this one unequal life all their eternal future. This is a paradox which offends both the soul and the reason, the ethical sense and the spiritual intuition."

Once we accept the idea of an eternal soul, it is essentially incumbent on us to recognize its past as well as its future. It is one thing to believe that life has no ultimate significance or future, and that the single birth is purely a chance of material creation, or an event in the All-Soul's development, thus making the life ephemeral and transitory. It is quite another to start from a creation out of material forces at the time of birth, and then build onto it an eternity of future result.

Essentially, if there is a recognition of a future, there must be concurrently a recognition of a past, and this brings in a process and a mechanism which provides the underpinning for the theory of rebirth and karma.

Sri Aurobindo, *Rebirth and Karma*, Section I, Chapter 4, Rebirth and Soul Evolution, pp. 32-33

Are Human Beings Fallen Celestial Beings?

Another theory that comes up is that the earth is somehow the penalty box for celestial beings who have "fallen" from their celestial status and they have the opportunity, through their efforts here to regain their celestial status. Even if there is some factual basis behind this supposition, clearly this still demands a past that influences the present circumstances, and a process, spanning potentially multiple rebirths, for the being to work through the "issues", as it is clear that one lifetime cannot and does not afford the celestial being the opportunity to solve the concerns so obviously visible when we look at the general "issues" with which humanity is burdened.

Sri Aurobindo explains his view on the matter: "But it is evident that this one earthly life is not sufficient for all to effect that difficult return, but rather most may and do miss it entirely; and we have then either to suppose that an immortal soul can perish or be doomed to eternal perdition or else that it has more existences than this poor precarious one apparently given to it, lives or states of being which intervene between its fall and the final working out of a sure redemption."

There are of course additional difficulties with this theory, not the least of which is the reason why this descent is necessary for all of these higher beings. There is also the rationale behind the differing conditions under which each of these beings is then asked to respond. "Each must surely have had a past which made him responsible for his present conditions, if he is to be held thus strictly to account for all their results and the use he makes of his often too scanty, grudging and sometimes quite hopeless opportunity. The very nature of our humanity supposes a varying constituent past for the soul as well as a resultant future."

We take away from this that whether the evolutionary process is completely of the earth, or involves souls moving between this and other worlds, there still is required a process and a mechanism for this soul evolution, and this therefore supports the process of rebirth and the working of karma.

Sri Aurobindo, *Rebirth and Karma*, Section I, Chapter 4, Rebirth and Soul Evolution, pg. 33

Does a Mental or Spiritual Being Form and Occupy the Physical Body?

There are those who try to understand the unique and powerful development of the human mind and spirit within the physical body by stating that the mental/spiritual personality waits for the development of the human being and then descends to occupy that formed instrument for its development and action from that point forward. That implies that the prior development that leads up to the human body, the physical and vital evolution, did not necessarily include a soul evolution. That evolution is said to begin with the descent once the human instrument has been prepared.

Sri Aurobindo inquires as to the mechanism and significance of this concept: "...what is it that brings about this connection of a spiritual being and higher mental nature and a physical being and lower animal nature? what necessitates this taking up of the lower life by the spirit which here becomes man? It would seem surely that there must have been some previous connection; the possessing mental or spiritual being must all the time have been preparing this lower life it thus occupies for a human manifestation. The whole evolution would then be an ordered continuity from the beginning and the intervention of mind and spirit would be no sudden inexplicable miracle, but a coming forward of that which was always there behind, an open taking up of the manifested life by a power which was always secretly presiding over the life evolution."

In essence, then, if we were to adopt this concept, there would not be any essential difference other than the locus occupied by the mental or spiritual being while the physical being was being developed. Whether that is here on the earth, or in some mental or spiritual plane, the mechanism is relatively the same for the evolutionary process to take place.

Sri Aurobindo, *Rebirth and Karma*, Section I, Chapter 4, Rebirth and Soul Evolution, pp. 33-34

Rebirth and Soul Evolution

Whether one accepts the idea of a fallen celestial being working out its salvation, or the concept of a mental/spiritual being forming and developing a physical body to inhabit and utilize for its ongoing development, the concept of rebirth appears to be necessary as a mechanism for this development. But neither of these two concepts actually addresses the meaning of the physical world and its structured organization and the apparent evolution of consciousness that appears to be the underlying thread tying all the levels of physical, vital and mental manifestation which we can observe. We do not need to posit such other-worldly solutions, although we also need not deny the possibilities, in order to put the process of rebirth squarely into the center of the development.

It is difficult for any of the "other world" explanations that rely on a single human birth to explain the varying issues, struggles and concerns that we face in the one lifetime.

"A past terrestrial soul evolution sufficiently accounting for these variations and degrees of our mixed being and a future soul evolution that helps us progressively to liberate the godhead of the spirit, seem the only just and reasonable explanation of this labour of a matter-shackled soul which has attained a variable degree of humanity in the midst of a general progressive appearance of the life, mind and spirit in a material universe. Rebirth is the only possible machinery for such a soul evolution."

Sri Aurobindo, *Rebirth and Karma*, Section I, Chapter 4, Rebirth and Soul Evolution, pp. 34-35

CHAPTER FIVE

THE SIGNIFICANCE OF REBIRTH

Seeking the Meaning of Human Life

Philosophy, religion and science all seek, in their own ways, for the meaning and purpose of our life on earth. The questions "why", "what" and "how" are the basis of this existential questioning of our existence. Where do we come from? Is there life before birth? Is there any existence after death, and if so, what is it?

Even if we try to avoid these questions and live a practical life of survival, or hedonistic enjoyment, they continue to impress themselves on thinking humanity. In mamy cases, those who have spent a lifetime denying this search for meaning, come in the end, on their death-beds, to the ultimate question with fear, trepidation, hope and prayer.

Sri Aurobindo provides an answer which addresses the various issues that arise: "In the idea of evolutionary rebirth, if we can once find it to be a truth and recognise its antecedents and consequences, we have a very sufficient clue for an answer to all these connected sides of the one perpetual question. A spiritual evolution of which our universe is the scene and earth its ground and stage, though its plan is still kept back above from our yet limited knowledge,–this way of seeing existence is a luminous key which we can fit into many doors of obscurity."

Sri Aurobindo places weight on the spiritual significance rather than the mechanical process. "The failure to do that rightly will involve us in much philosophical finessing, drive on this side or the other to exaggerated negations and leave our statement of it, however perfect may be its logic, yet unsatisfying and unconvincing to the total intelligence and the complex soul of humanity."

Sri Aurobindo, *Rebirth and Karma*, Section I, Chapter 5, The Significance of Rebirth, pg. 35

The Finality of Death Is Overcome By Rebirth

When we confront the issues of our bodily life, the prospect of rebirth provides us with a sense of continuity and at least some response to the finality of the death of the body. We gain a sense that we have been born before, and that after we die, something will continue and be born yet again.

The impact on our psyche of overcoming death in any manner should not be underestimated. This is the "great fear" that we carry with us all through our lives, and anything that promises us an extension or continuance in some form is generally welcomed.

Sri Aurobindo picks up on this theme: " For the burden of death to man the thinking, willing, feeling creature is not the loss of this poor case or chariot of body, but it is the blind psychical finality death suggests, the stupid material end of our will and thought and aspiration and endeavour, the brute breaking off of the heart's kind and sweet relations and affections, the futile convicting discontinuity of that marvelous and all-supporting soul-sense which gives us our radiant glimpses of the glory and delight of existence,–that is the discord and harsh inconsequence against which the thinking living creature revolts as incredible and inadmissible. The fiery straining to immortality of our life, mind, psyche, which can assent to cessation only by turning in enmity upon their own flame of nature, and the denial of it which the dull acquiescence of a body consenting inertly to death as to life brings in on us, is the whole painful irreconcilable contradiction of our double nature. Rebirth takes the difficulty and solves it in the sense of a soul continuity with a beat of physical repetition."

There is, however, in this baseline analysis, not yet any sense of purpose of this mechanical repetition of birth, death, and rebirth; nor do we have any clear sense of "who" or "what" it is that experiences the rebirth. These questions continue to intrigue us.

"But simple persistence, mechanical continuity is not enough; that is not all our physical being signifies, not the whole luminous meaning of survival and continuity; without ascension, without expansion, without some growing up straight into light in the strength of our spirit our higher members toil here uncompleted, our birth in matter is not justified by any adequate meaning. We are very little better off than if death remained our ending; for our life in the end becomes then an indefinitely continued and renewed and temporarily consequent in place of an inconsequent, abruptly ended and soon convicted futility."

Sri Aurobindo, *Rebirth and Karma*, Section I, Chapter 5, The Significance of Rebirth, pp. 35-36

A Soul Evolution Uses Rebirth As Its Mechanism of Fulfilment

Rebirth, if restricted to the physical mechanism, adds little meaning to our lives, as it becomes an endless repetition of births with no goal other than pure existence. This leaves the questions about the significance of life and the reason for existence unanswered. Once we couple this physical mechanism with the concept of a soul evolution, a continuously progressive development that utilizes rebirth as the means of achieving results that cannot be attained in any single birth, we have the key that fits virtually all the locks, and we open up a new understanding about why we are here, and what we have to do.

Sri Aurobindo states the case in a concise manner: "But the perception of rebirth as an occasion and means for a spiritual evolution fills in every hiatus. It makes life a significant ascension and not a mechanical recurrence; it opens to us the divine vistas of a growing soul; it makes the worlds a nexus of spiritual self-expansion; it sets us seeking, and with a sure promise to all of a great finding now or hereafter, for the self-knowledge of our spirit and the self-fulfilment of a wise and divine intention in our existence."

Sri Aurobindo, *Rebirth and Karma*, Section I, Chapter 5, The Significance of Rebirth, pp. 37-38

The Futility of a Purely Mechanical Process of Rebirth

If the entire meaning of rebirth is a physical reincarnation, with no other significance, goal or purpose, we eventually come to the point of asking "what for?". Why go through the struggle, the suffering, the repeated births, lives and deaths, only to be reborn again into a similar circumstance, like a hamster running in a never-ending wheel. Many who achieve the recognition of the reality of rebirth, but who do not see any higher purpose, conclude eventually that the entire round of births and deaths and the chain of karma are futile, and they reach an existential crisis. This crisis in fact was the underlying force behind the rise of existentialism in the West, with its air of the unreality of our world, the meaninglessness of it, and the overwhelming physical revulsion expressed by them as "nausea".

In the East, Buddhism focused on this repetitive round of births and deaths and the suffering that accompanied it, and determined that a solution was to free oneself from it entirely.

Sri Aurobindo describes the view of the physical rebirth mechanism: "What we see in the material universe is a stupendous system of mechanical recurrences. A huge mechanical recurrence rules that which is long-enduring and vast; a similar but frailer mechanical recurrence sways all that is ephemeral and small. The suns leap up into being, flame wheeling in space, squander force by motion and fade and are extinct, again perhaps to blaze into being and repeat their course, or else other suns take their place and fulfil their round. The seasons of Time repeat their unending and unchanging cycle. Always the tree of life puts forth its various flowers and sheds them and breaks into the same flowers in their recurring season. The body of man is born and grows and decays and perishes, but it gives birth to other bodies which maintain the one same futile cycle. What baffles the intelligence in all this intent and persistent process is that it seems to have in it no soul of meaning, no significance except the simple fact of causeless and purposeless existence dogged or relieved by the annulling or the compensating fact of individual cessation. And this is because we perceive the mechanism, but do not see the Power that uses the mechanism and the intention in its use. But the moment we know that there is a conscious Spirit self-wise and infinite brooding upon the universe and a secret slowly self-finding soul in things, we get to the necessity of an idea in its consciousness, a thing conceived, willed, set in motion and securely to be done, progressively to be fulfilled by these great deliberate workings."

Sri Aurobindo, *Rebirth and Karma*, Section I, Chapter 5, The Significance of Rebirth, pp. 38-39

Implications of the Buddhist Approach to Rebirth

The Buddhist approaches recognizes rebirth as well as karma. It starts from the mechanical recurrence proposition for the physical existence, and recognizes that there is an energy that propels this rebirth process forward according to the chain of cause and effect, karma. Buddhism however does not accept nor recognize any eternity to the soul; rather it treats the soul much in the same way it treats the body, as a phenomenon of the mechanical cause and effect which acts based on the desire-will.

Sri Aurobindo describes it thus: "As this constant hereditary succession of lives is a prolongation of the one universal principle of life by a continued creation of similar bodies, a mechanical recurrence, so the system of soul rebirth too is a constant prolongation of the principle of the soul-life by a continued creation through Karma of similar embodied associations and experiences, a mechanical recurrence. As the cause of all this physical birth and long hereditary continuation is an obscure will to life in Matter, so the cause of continued soul birth is an ignorant desire or will to be in the universal energy of Karma. As the constant wheelings of the universe and the motions of its forces generate individual existences who escape from or end in being by an individual dissolution, so there is this constant wheel of becoming and motion of Karma which forms into individualised soul-lives that must escape from their continuity by a dissolving cessation. An extinction of the embodied consciousness is our apparent material end; for soul too the end is extinction, the blank satisfaction of Nothingness or some ineffable bliss of a superconscient Non-Being. The affirmation of the mechanical occurrence or recurrence of birth is the essence of this view; but while the bodily life suffers an enforced end and dissolution, the soul life ceases by a willed self-extinction."

The Buddhist view is, in its own right, an enormous progress from the view that treats life and physical existence purely as consisting of an essentially meaningless procession of days ending in death with no purpose or significance; but it does not yet provide us any affirmative rationale for the existence of the universe and the entire structure of life and being.

Sri Aurobindo, *Rebirth and Karma*, Section I, Chapter 5, The Significance of Rebirth, pp. 39-40

Implications of the Illusionist (Mayavada) Approach to Rebirth

The starting point for the illusionist view of rebirth is in many respects similar to the starting point of the Buddhist view. The mechanical process of rebirth, ever-repeating the same basic round of birth, life and death is the underlying experience. As with the Buddhist view, also, there is a sense that this mechanical round is something to be escaped or liberated from. Where it differs to some degree is the understanding it brings to what happens after successfully achieving that liberation. The illusionist view holds out that there is a Reality that exists separate and apart from this world of illusion and that upon liberation, we eternally partake of that Reality.

As with the Buddhist view, it treats the world of life that we normally experience as something either unreal and illusory, and our effort needs to be to disentangle ourselves from this present external life and world so as to achieve the liberation.

Sri Aurobindo points out that such a view does not provide any answer to the question of "why" there should be an external world within which we live if there is no ultimate meaning or reality to it. He quotes from the Koran when he cites: "Thinkest thou that I have made the heavens and the earth and all that is between them in a jest?"

While the soul, burdened by the experience of suffering and the sense of the unreality of the world, experiences a relief when it finally escapes, this does not actually resolve the cosmic riddle, simply avoids it.

Sri Aurobindo describes the issue: "But it gives no real, because no fruitful answer to the problem of God and man and the significance of life; it only gets away from them by a skilful evasion and takes away from them all significance, so that any question of the sense and will in all this tremendous labour and throb and seeking loses meaning. But the challenge of God's universe to the knowledge and strength of the human spirit cannot in the end be met by man with a refusal or solved by an evasion, even though an individual soul may take refuge from the demand, as a man may from the burden of action and pain in unconsciousness, in spiritual trance or sleep or escape through its blank doors into the Absolute. Something the Spirit of the universe means by our labour in existence, some sense it has in these grandiose rhythms, and it has not undertaken them in an eternally enduring error or made them in a jest. To know that and possess it, to find and fulfil consciously the universal being's hidden significances is the task given to the human spirit."

Sri Aurobindo, *Rebirth and Karma*, Section I, Chapter 5, The Significance of Rebirth, pp. 40-41

Implications of the Vaishnava Viewpoint on Rebirth

We have seen the mechanical process of rebirth, and we have reviewed solutions that essentially treat the world as either an illusion or a field of suffering, to be escaped or liberated from. Neither of these solutions proposes any real and positive significance to the human life that we experience in this world of struggle. They each seek a solution that eventually avoids this world. Sri Aurobindo has pointed out that these solutions do not represent the complete key to our existence, and until we find a real significance to our life, we must assume that something is still missing from our understanding.

The Vaishnava path of Hinduism provides the first glimmer of a positive sense to existence, by proposing that life is a divine play of the divine Being and the goal is to manifest and experience that divine Bliss. Sri Aurobindo finds this positive affirmation to be both powerful and insightful. At the same time, he indicates that it has not gone quite far enough:

"There is more here in the world than a play of secret delight; there is knowledge, there is power, there is a will and a mighty labour. Rebirth so looked at becomes too much of a divine caprice with no object but its playing, and ours is too great and strenuous a world to be so accounted for."

Sri Aurobindo, *Rebirth and Karma*, Section I, Chapter 5, The Significance of Rebirth, pg. 42

Implications of the
Tantric Viewpoint on Rebirth

Tantra focuses on the energy of creation, the Divine Shakti, and its manifestation through the world of forms. Tantra provides a first basis for a serious potential significance to life and rebirth. Sri Aurobindo describes the tantric perspective: "The Tantric solution shows us a supreme superconscient Energy which casts itself out here into teeming worlds and multitudinous beings and in its order the soul rises from birth to birth and follows its million forms, till in a last human series it opens to the consciousness and powers of its own divinity and returns through them by a rapid illumination to the eternal superconscience."

We can see here the essence of the idea of an evolution of forms, and a progressive embodiment of ever higher levels of consciousness in these successively developed forms. We see here a real potential value and meaning to the life and struggle we experience in the universe. The tantric proposition thus approaches a solution that can answer all the questions and concerns.

Where the tantric approach is still incomplete is that it still posits as the eventual goal the abandonment of life into a supreme superconscience, so that eventually the significance it attributes to life is ephemeral and temporary in nature. Sri Aurobindo points out that "We find at last the commencement of a satisfying synthesis, some justification of existence, a meaningful consequence in rebirth, a use and a sufficient though only temporary significance for the great motion of the cosmos."

The difficulty remaining is essentially that there is obviously so much consciousness, energy, effort and organization involved in the manifestation of the universe that we still cannot find it sufficient as a rationale for all of this, that the goal remains one of "escape". As Sri Aurobindo points out: "...the supreme Energy constructs too long and stupendous a preparation for so brief and so insufficient a flowering."

Sri Aurobindo, *Rebirth and Karma*, Section I, Chapter 5, The Significance of Rebirth, pg. 42

Evolutionary Rebirth and the Meaning of Life

Sri Aurobindo's guiding principle in his review of rebirth is to ensure that he answers the major issues and questions that revolve around both the process and the significance. This implies that we recognize the reality and purpose of the material universe and not simply try to dismiss it as an illusion or something that must be escaped from.

One of the greatest obstacles to finding a suitable solution is our tendency to remain fixated on the world as we see it today and to extrapolate both backwards and forwards in a static, rather than a dynamic, manner. Thus, we believe the current status of life and conscious awareness will continue as it is into the future and we have a hard time recognizing or visualizing a future that is greater than and significantly different than what we see as our opportunities and limits today.

Sri Aurobindo's vision moves us out of these restrictions: "But what if rebirth were in truth no long dragging chain, but rather at first a ladder of the soul's ascension and at last a succession of mighty spiritual opportunities? It will be so if the infinite existence is not what it seems to the logical intellect, an abstract entity, but what it is to intuition and in deeper soul experience, a conscious spiritual Reality, and that Reality as real here as in any far off absolute Superconscience. For then universal Nature would be no longer a mechanism with no secret but its own inconscient mechanics and no intention but the mere recurrent working; it would be the conscient energy of the universal Spirit hidden in the greatness of its processes, *mahimanam asya.*"And the soul ascending from the sleep of matter through plant and animal life to the human degree of the power of life and there battling with ignorance and limit to take possession of its royal and infinite kingdom would be the mediator appointed to unfold in Nature the spirit who is hidden in her subtleties and her vastnesses. That is the significance of life and the world which the idea of evolutionary rebirth opens to us; life becomes at once a progressive ascending series for the unfolding of the Spirit. It acquires a supreme significance: the way of the Spirit in its power is justified, no longer a foolish and empty dream, an eternal delirium, great mechanical toil or termless futility, but the sum of works of a large spiritual Will and Wisdom: the human soul and the cosmic spirit look into each other's eyes with a noble and divine meaning."

Sri Aurobindo, *Rebirth and Karma*, Section I, Chapter 5, The Significance of Rebirth, pp. 42-43

The Soul, Spiritual Evolution and the Meaning of Life

In a brief compass, Sri Aurobindo integrates the soul and the universe into a coherent and significant process of Reality: "What we are is a soul of the transcendent Spirit and Self unfolding itself in the cosmos in a constant evolutionary embodiment of which the physical side is only a pedestal of form corresponding in its evolution to the ascending degrees of the spirit, but the spiritual growth is the real sense and motive."

The past represents the prior stages of this evolution of consciousness in form. The present represents a stage in that evolution which has not yet been completed. The future holds the next stages and opens up the evolutionary development to new and greater manifestations of consciousness.

Our purpose in existence then is to act as a nexus of this increasing development of the spiritual evolution: "Why we are here is to be this means of the spirit's upward self-unfolding. What we have to do with ourselves and our significances is to grow and open them to greater significances of divine being, divine consciousness, divine power, divine delight and multiplied unity, and what we have to do with our environment is to use it consciously for increasing spiritual purposes and make it more and more a mould for the ideal unfolding of the perfect nature and self-conception of the Divine in the cosmos."

Sri Aurobindo has encapsulated here the essence of our striving and search for meaning. This provides not only a sense of the Reality of the material universal manifestation, but also a real purpose and meaning to the struggles for growth and aspiration for consciousness that we see within ourselves, and provides a significance to the process of rebirth as an essential mechanism for the successive growth of the soul and its ability to more and more effectively manifest the consciousness of the Spirit in matter, life and mind.

Sri Aurobindo, *Rebirth and Karma*, Section I, Chapter 5, The Significance of Rebirth, pp. 43-44

Comparison of Rebirth
With Other Theories of Existence

To the mind limited by the scope of our daily existence and understanding, rebirth is one among any number of theories, but not something settled. Sri Aurobindo points out that even from the viewpoint of the mental perspective, which weighs possibilities and probabilities, but cannot come to any certain conclusions, the theory of rebirth explains the facts of our existence at least as well as the other theories being entertained: "...it is a better hypothesis than the naive and childlike religious solutions which make the world an arbitrary caprice and man the breathing clay puppet of an almighty human-minded Creator, and at least as good a hypothesis as the idea of a material inconscient Force somehow stumbling into a precarious, ephemeral, yet always continued phenomenon of consciousness, or a creative Life labouring in the Bergsonian formula oppressed but constant in the midst of a universal death, as good too as the idea of a mechanical working of Prakriti, Maya, Shakti into which or in which a real or unreal individual stumbles and wanders,... until he can get out of it by a spiritual liberation."

The crux of the issue is whether the human being is a static creation fixed forever in its place, or an evolutionary being with dynamic potential to develop beyond the level of consciousness we currently are able to manifest. Rebirth provides a mechanism for dynamic development, which is not required in a static universe.

"Its truth will depend on spiritual experience and effectuation; but chiefly on this momentous issue, whether there is anything in the soul-powers of man which promises a greater term of being than his present mentality and whether that greater term can be made effective for his embodied existence? That is the question which remains over to be tested by psychological inquiry and the problem to be resolved in the course of the spiritual evolution of man."

Sri Aurobindo, *Rebirth and Karma*, Section I, Chapter 5, The Significance of Rebirth, pp. 44-45

Rebirth and the Ladder of Spiritual Evolution

The necessity of rebirth hinges on the ultimate meaning of the manifestation of the universe. If it is random chance, or purely mechanical machinery, there is no necessity of rebirth. If, on the other hand, there is a conscious Will and Purpose to the universe, and the human being is part of that purpose and carrying out an evolutionary role, then rebirth becomes a centerpiece of the process.

Sri Aurobindo discusses these issues: "Once we find that there is a conscious Spirit of which this movement is one expression, or even admit that as our working hypothesis, we are bound to go on and ask whether this developing order ceases with what man now is or is laden with something more towards which it and he have to grow, an unfinished expression, a greater unfound term, and in that case it is evidently towards that greater thing that man must be growing; to prepare it and to realise it must be the stage beyond in his destiny. Towards that new step in the evolution his history as a race must be subconsciously tending and the powers of the highest individuals half consciently striving to be delivered of this greater birth; and since the ascending order of rebirth follows always the degrees of the evolution, that too cannot be meant to stop short or shoot off abruptly into the superconscient without any regard to the intended step."

If we find that man is therefore a "transitional being", as Sri Aurobindo has described elsewhere, then we can explore the "ladder of evolution" both with respect to the prior steps of the ascent of consciousness out of involvement in Matter, through the progressive development of Life, and the subsequent stages of expression of Mind, as well as the future stages beyond our current mental development into what Sri Aurobindo describes as the "supramental" ranges of consciousness.

"The whole processional significance of rebirth may be wrapped up in that one yet unattempted discovery."

Sri Aurobindo, *Rebirth and Karma*, Section I, Chapter 5, The Significance of Rebirth, pp. 45-46

CHAPTER SIX

THE ASCENDING UNITY

The Simple and the Complex

There is a concept in philosophy known as Occam's Razor which holds, essentially, that if all other things are equal, the simplest explanation is likely to be the correct one. This concept helps cut through the layers of complexity that confront us when we try to understand the world around us and the role we play in it. There are benefits to this concept when it helps us avoid complexity that is simply developed by the human mind for the sake of apparent profundity, or for the purpose of baffling and misleading others.

At the same time, if we gaze with a clear vision at the world around us, we find that the "simplest" is frequently not fully able to address the reality of the universe.

Humans prefer simple explanations and thus, favor responses that are "black and white" rather than those that have subtlety and complexity of interactive and inter-related parts.

Nevertheless, the real world is not as simple as we may choose to view it. Whether we view the structure of the material universe and the action of subatomic particles, the inter-relationships of the innumerable forms of living beings in a symbiotic living web, or we view the human body with its numerous interactive organ systems and physiological functions that involve very finely tuned biochemical reactions, we find complexity everywhere. To truly understand the world and our lives, we therefore must be prepared to develop our understanding to both encompass simplicity to cut through verbal convoluted structures, and complexity when viewing the refined intelligence of the organisation of the universe.

Sri Aurobindo prefaces the new chapter with some thoughts on this issue: "But after all perhaps when we come to think more at large about the matter, we may find that Nature and Existence are not of the same mind as man in this respect, that there is here a great complexity which we must follow with patience and that those ways of thinking have most chance of a fruitful truth-yielding, which like the inspired thinking of the Upanishads take in many sides at once and reconcile many conflicting conclusions."

As we move from a world-view that is both anthropocentric and earth-centric, to one that recognizes the much larger ecosphere, bio-sphere and universe, we find that a global or even a universal view vastly expands our vision and understanding as we recognise and embrace more aspects of the universal creation.

Sri Aurobindo, *Rebirth and Karma*, Section I, Chapter 6, The Ascending Unity, pp. 47-48

Overcoming the Tendency to Over-Simplification

The mind loves to make distinctions and separate things into categories. This tendency starts with our own individuality as we distinguish between the human being and the world around us. The planet, plants, animals are all treated as something else, something other and we then objectify them and look upon them as if they are created for our individual use and enjoyment. Similarly we extend this view to put our world at the center of universal creation. The suns, planets, stars are thus created just for us. Even if we do not exactly comprehend the purpose behind this massive machinery, we nevertheless tend to treat it as a background or a stage for our lives to unfold.

Even when we recognize the universal existence, it is generally in contra-distinction to the individual life and we then attribute reality to either the one side or the other, and focus our attention either on the universal or the individual.

The result here is that we tend to over-simplify things by focusing on the distinctions rather than the unity that embraces and contains all the diversity and separations. Sri Aurobindo concludes: "Our classifications set up too rigid walls; all borders are borders only and not impassable gulfs. The one infinitely variable Spirit in things carries over all of himself into each form of his omnipresence; the self, the Being is at once unique in each, common in our collectivities and one in all beings. God moves in many ways at once in his own indivisible unity."

The Reality of existence is comprehensive, encompassing both the individual forms and their inter-relations, as well as the universal and Transcendent that make them all part of one larger Oneness. The truth of the individual cannot truly be understood without taking into account the universal creation. And neither can be fully appreciated without integrating the Transcendent.

Sri Aurobindo, *Rebirth and Karma*, Section I, Chapter 6, The Ascending Unity, pp. 48-49

Humanity Represents a Continuum in Life's Development in the World

If we put aside for the moment religious or philosophical dogma and simply look at the world around us and our position within it, we can see that humanity did not simply "appear" without "context". Sri Aurobindo describes the relationship to the rest of creation thus: "The animal prepares and imperfectly prefigures man and is itself prepared in the plant, as that too is foreseen obscurely by all that precedes it in the terrestrial expansion. Man himself takes up the miraculous play of the electron and atom, draws up through the complex development of the protoplasm the chemical life of subvital beings, perfects the original nervous system of the plant in the physiology of the completed animal being, consummates and repeats rapidly in his embryonic growth the past evolution of the animal form into the human perfection and, once born, rears himself from the earthward and downward animal proneness to the erect figure of the spirit who is already looking up to his farther heavenward evolution. All the terrestrial past of the world is there summarised in man, and not only has Nature given as it were the physical sign that she has formed in him an epitome of her universal forces, but psychologically also he is one in his subconscient being with her obscurer animal life, contains in his mind and nature the animal and rises out of all this substratum into his conscious manhood."

Not only is there an obvious continuum here which places the human being squarely in the midst of the evolutionary process of the world, but there is also a clearly symbiotic relationship that makes it impossible for the human being to live without the environment and the other beings in the environment to support, nurture and create the conditions needed for our existence. We require oxygen to breathe, and plants create oxygen. We have beneficial bacteria in our intestines that are important to our digestive process. Our skin creates an essential vitamin from sun rays. The entire creation is One and unified and depends on each part to manifest the whole.

Sri Aurobindo, *Rebirth and Karma*, Section I, Chapter 6, The Ascending Unity, pp. 49-50

Does the Soul Exist in Subhuman Nature?

Admitting the unity and integrated oneness of the physical creation, there remain those who attempt nevertheless to assert that the soul or spiritual nature is something separate and distinct and thereby unique in mankind. This however goes against the entire picture we see of a systematic outflowering and evolution of consciousness out of Matter, through Life and Mind (and beyond). The soul should follow a similar evolutionary curve and process of development. Otherwise, what is the sense and meaning of the material evolution?

Sri Aurobindo indicates: "...it is reasonable to suppose that whatever has been the past history of the individual soul, it must have followed the course of the universal nature and evolution."

"The physical history of humankind is the growth out of the subvital and the animal life into the greater power of manhood; our inner history as indicated by our present nature, which is the animal plus something that exceeds it, must have been a simultaneous and companion growing on the same curve into the soul of humanity. The ancient Indian idea which refused to separate nature of man from the universal Nature or self of man from the one common self, accepted this consequence of its seeing. Thus the Tantra assigns eighty millions of plant and animal lives as the sum of the preparation for a human birth and, without binding ourselves to the figure, we can appreciate the force of its idea of the difficult soul evolution by which humanity has come or perhaps constantly comes into being. We can only get away from this necessity of an animal past by denying all soul to subhuman nature."

Sri Aurobindo, *Rebirth and Karma*, Section I, Chapter 6, The Ascending Unity, pg. 50

The Soul, Karma and the Evolutionary Progression

The law of karma as part of a process of soul evolution and development can only have meaning if it is continuous and follows the line of development. This implies that it is active in the pre-human evolutionary stages as well as in the human and beyond. This then implies that the soul exists, not only as a unique "creation" dropped into human life, but in the pre-human evolutionary stages as well. It appears that the soul develops and evolves in sync with the external evolutionary development.

Sri Aurobindo discusses the issue: "Because soul or spirit works in the animal on a lower scale, we are not warranted in thinking that there is no soul in him, any more than a divine or superhuman being would be justified in regarding us as soulless bodies or soulless minds because of the grovelling downward drawn inferiority of our half-animal nature."

"The spiritual law of Karma is that the nature of each being can be only the result of his past energies; to suppose a soul which assumes and continues a past karma that is not its own, is to cut a line of dissociation across this law and bring in an unknown and unverified factor. But if we admit it, we must account for that factor, we must explain or discover by what law, by what connection, by what necessity, by what strange impulsion of choice a spirit pure of all animal nature assumes a body and nature of animality prepared for it by a lower order of being. If there is no affinity and no consequence of past identity or connection, this becomes an unnatural and impossible assumption. Then it is the most reasonable and concordant conclusion that man has the animal nature...because the developing self in him like the developed body has had a past subhuman evolution. This conclusion preserves the unity of Nature and its developing order; and it concurs with the persistent evidence of an interaction and parallelism which we perceive between the inward and the outward, the physical and the mental phenomenon...."

"...it makes soul or spirit, no longer a miraculous accident or intervention in a material universe, but a constant presence in it and the secret of its order and its existence."

Sri Aurobindo, *Rebirth and Karma*, Section I, Chapter 6, The Ascending Unity, pp. 50-52

The Soul and Subhuman Existence

In ancient times, the world was invested with spirit everywhere, in all things. Sri Aurobindo describes it thus: "Ancient belief...saw a soul, a living godhead everywhere in the animate and in the inanimate and nothing was to its view void of a spiritual existence."

The development of the logical mind and its focus on dividing, classifying and simplifying through trenchant separation rejected this view of life. It does not mean, however, that this is the final answer to the question.

Sri Aurobindo describes a process of development that is one unified continuum, and this implies that soul exists, in some form, not only in the human and the animal existence, but even in the earlier, more primitive forms of life. "...it is now clear that the nervous life which is the basis of that physical mentality in man and animal, exists also in the plant with a fundamental identity; not only so, but it is akin to us by a sort of nervous psychology which amounts to the existence of a suppressed mind. A subconscient mind in the plant, it is now not unreasonable to suggest,–but is it not at the summits of plant experience only half subconscious?–becomes conscient in the animal body. When we go lower down, we find hints that there are involved in the subvital most brute material forms the rudiments of precisely the same energy of life and its responses."

The work of Dr. Bose on the consciousness of plants, and those who have followed in his footsteps, has documented "The Secret Life of Plants" and there can be now little doubt of the scientific support for the existence of consciousness and responsiveness in animals and plants. Further work with crystals and minerals has even begun to uncover the responsiveness that Sri Aurobindo has posited in the world of material forms.

One consciousness, one existence, in a unity that spans from the most inconscient Matter to the heights of Spirit, implies that there is a continuum and our attempt to divide and classify and separate is an artificial mental construct but not an essential underlying Reality of the manifested universe.

We find that the ancient view of inclusion has more ultimate truth in it that the modern view of fragmentation.

Sri Aurobindo, *Rebirth and Karma*, Section I, Chapter 6, The Ascending Unity, pg. 52

Birth Of the Spirit Into Form

If the manifestation of the universal creation is one unbroken unity expressing a spiritual evolution of consciousness which is involved in Matter and progressively reveals itself in ever-increasing forms of consciousness, then there is no division or separation of "soul" or "spirit" apart from "matter" or "life".

Sri Aurobindo refers to the Vedic word: "…out of all the ocean of inconscience…it is that one spiritual Existent who is born by the greatness of his own energy…"

The soul then must always be there, even in the most inconscient forms of Matter, involved, but present, waiting for the preparation of the form required to make itself known and be recognized.

Sri Aurobindo addresses the mystical reality this way: "We come to a fathomless conception of this all, *sarvam idam,* in which we see that there is an obscure omnipresent life in matter, activised by that life a secret sleeping mind, sheltered in that sleep of mind an involved all-knowing all-originating Spirit."

"All assumption of form is a constant and yet progressive birth or becoming of the soul, *sambhava, sambhuti,*–the dumb and blind and brute is that and not only the finely, mentally conscious human or the animal existence. All this infinite becoming is a birth of the Spirit into form. This is the truth, obscure at first or vague to the intelligence, but very luminous to an inner experience, on which the ancient Indian idea of rebirth took its station."

Sri Aurobindo, *Rebirth and Karma*, Section I, Chapter 6, The Ascending Unity, pp. 52-54

Universal and Individual Are
Two Poles of One Unified Existence

Just as the fragmentation of creation through the ego conscious-ness is artificial and unreal in the overarching unity of existence, so too the other extreme position of unity with no separateness of forms and purposes is artificial and denies a truth of the creation. Sri Aurobindo's viewpoint is one that embraces unity and diver-sity without them being in contradiction to one another; rather, they are both aspects and important elements of the creation. The unity provides the foundation and the harmony of the larger whole, while the diversification of forms allows a unique creation to manifest and develop into innumerable relations.

Without this dynamic relationship of the One with the Many, we would be hard-pressed to find a rationale for the individual and the systematic evolutionary development of the individual and thus, the process of rebirth and the role of karma.

Sri Aurobindo expounds on this point: "Individuality is as im-portant a thing to the ways of the Spirit of existence as universal-ity. The individual is that potent secret of its being upon which the universal stresses and leans and makes the knot of power of all its workings: as the individual grows in consciousness and sight and knowledge and all divine power and quality, increasingly he becomes aware of the universal in himself, but aware of himself too in the universality, of his own past not begun and ended in the single transient body, but opening to future consummations. If the aim of the universal in our birth is to become self-conscient and possess and enjoy its being, still it is done through the indi-vidual's flowering and perfection; if to escape from its own work-ings be the last end, still it is the individual that escapes while the universal seems content to continue its multitudinous births to all eternity. Therefore the individual would appear to be a real power of the Spirit and not a simple illusion or device, except in so far as the universal too may be, as some would have it, an immense illusion or a grand imposed device. On this line of thinking we arrive at the idea of some great spiritual existence of which uni-versal and individual are two companion powers, pole and pole of its manifestation, indefinite circumference and multiple centre of the activised realities of its being."

Sri Aurobindo, *Rebirth and Karma*, Section I, Chapter 6, The Ascending Unity, pp. 54-55

An Ascending Unity As the Basis for Rebirth

Sri Aurobindo summarizes the discussion of this chapter to provide a straightforward and logical presentation of the development of consciousness through ever-ascending forms, providing a rationale and basis for the theory of rebirth. In this summary he has addressed the major facts of our existence and the primary issues that arise as to the significance of life and the reasons why rebirth is an essential element of this development.

"This is a way of seeing things, harmonious at least in its complexity, supple and capable of a certain all-embracing scope, which we can take as a basis for our ideas of rebirth,–an ascending unity, a spirit involved in material existence which scales wonderfully up many gradations through life to organised mind and beyond mind to the evolution of its own complete self-conscience, the individual following that gradation and the power for its self-crowning."

There are various possibilities for this development which may include any of the major theories of existence that have come to the fore during mankind's search for meaning. "If human mind is the last word of its possibility on earth, then rebirth must end in man and proceed by some abrupt ceasing either to an existence on other planes or to an annulment of its spiritual circle. But if there are higher powers of the spirit which are attainable by birth, then the ascent is not finished, greater assumptions may lie before the soul which has now reached and is lifted to a perfecting of the high scale of humanity."

What higher opportunities or heights may reach beyond our human stage of manifestation, remains to be seen and discovered. There is always the "Eternal's infinite potentiality."

Sri Aurobindo, *Rebirth and Karma*, Section I, Chapter 6, The Ascending Unity, pg. 55

Chapter Seven

Involution and Evolution

Modern and Ancient Views of Evolution

The first thing we think about when the topic of evolution comes up is the modern scientific approach and viewpoint. Evolution in the scientific world is a process which describes a mechanism that brings about ever new and systematically developing forms of life. In and of itself, the Western viewpoint does not assign any particular ultimate meaning or significance to evolution and is content to describe the process and uncover facts that are essentially details of that process.

There is however another, a more ancient view of evolution, propounded by the ancient seers and sages of India. This view focuses more on the inner spiritual significance of the process rather than just the external details. The Sankhya thinker "... saw in it too not only the covering active evident Force, but the concealed sustaining spiritual entity...." Sri Aurobindo points out that the Sankhya thinker "...had no eye for the detail of the physical labour of Nature." Additionally, he set up a gulf between Spirit and the Force of physical evolution.

On the other hand, Sri Aurobindo describes the modern view of evolution: "The modern scientist strives to make a complete scheme and institution of the physical method which he has detected in its minute workings, but is blind to the miracle each step involves or content to lose the sense of it in the satisfied observation of a vast ordered phenomenon." The scientist misses the miracle, the "inexplicable wonder of all existence..."

Sri Aurobindo points out that each of these starting points provides us a relevant insight, but neither of them has the complete picture. "We know that an evolution there is, but not what evolution is; that remains still one of the initial mysteries of Nature."

Sri Aurobindo, *Rebirth and Karma*, Section I, Chapter 7, Involution and Evolution, pp. 56-57

Evolution and Creation

There has been a long-standing divergence between "religion" and "science", in particular surrounding the questions of "creation" versus "evolution". On the one side, there is the sense that there is some superior or external Power (God, the Creator, etc.) which has created this entire universe and all its forms out of "nothing" or out of its own "substance", and the specific details of the creation are subordinated to the miraculous nature of it. On the other side, there is a strong focus on the process of it, and the details of the multi-billion year systematic development of the universe and its forms from the time of the "big bang" to today, with the development of innumerable specific forms arising out of the energy and matter of the universe going through systematic combinations are what command the entire attention.

The evolutionists have no answer to the question of "how" or "why" or "in what manner" the initial start of this process occurred, and it is at this point that a potential resolution of this long-standing conflict may actually be found.

Sri Aurobindo describes the remaining question that must be the subject of our human inquiry: "The way in which man sees and experiences the universe, imposes on his reason the necessity of a one original eternal substance of which all things are the forms and a one eternal original energy of which all movement of action and consequence is the variation. But the whole question is what is the reality of this substance and what is the essential nature of this energy?"

Until we address this question, we cannot find a resolution of the debate between "evolution" and "creation" as theories of existence.

Sri Aurobindo, *Rebirth and Karma*, Section I, Chapter 7, Involution and Evolution, pp. 57-58

A Spiritual Evolution Is the Key To the Universal Manifestation

Without some deeper significance, the development of life out of matter, and mind out of life is certainly inexplicable. How does inanimate Matter develop Life? How does Mind develop out of Life? What about the expression of the Soul? We are left with nothing to answer this without resorting to a "miraculous creation" by an external all-knowing, all-powerful Creator (which itself brings up any number of inexplicable issues), or we are left with the action of random chance combining together elements and chemicals and haphazardly thereby yielding up ever-increasing forms of Consciousness.

Sri Aurobindo's provides a solution by his understanding that each form and level of consciousness that evolves out must have been "involved" to begin with. Behind each of these newly expressed levels of consciousness, there is an involved energy that manifests itself when the conditions become appropriate. One can see that when one plants an acorn in the ground, an oak tree will result, if the proper conditions of soil, climate, temperature, moisture are available to allow the development. Scientists studying the process of seed formation and germination eventually have shown that the seed encodes the specific powers and forms of that specific being, whether plant or animal. This is the physical correspondence to the involution of consciousness that Sri Aurobindo is describing.

Sri Aurobindo concludes that "...Nature [is] only the force of self-expression, self-formation, self-creation of a secret spirit, and man however hedged in his present capacity, [is] the first being in Nature in whom that power begins to be consciently self-creative in the front of the action, in this outer chamber of the physical being, there set to work and bring out by an increasingly self-conscious evolution what he can of all its human significance or its divine possibility..." This is the result of concluding that "...the reality of this whole mounting creation [is] a spiritual evolution."

Sri Aurobindo, *Rebirth and Karma*, Section I, Chapter 7, Involution and Evolution, pp. 58-59

The Spirit Involved In Matter

If we once recognize the oneness of the entire manifested universe and see that there is a systematic evolution of consciousness that takes place through a concurrent ever-evolving series of forms, then it is easily concluded that what has evolved must have been involved in the first place. The spiritual principle, then, is involved in Matter, similar to the example cited previously of the acorn holding the essential nature of the oak tree within it, allow it to manifest when placed into appropriately supportive circumstance.

Sri Aurobindo discusses this issue as follows: "We are bound then to suppose that all that evolves already existed involved, passive or otherwise active, but in either case concealed from us in the shell of material Nature. The Spirit which manifests itself here in a body, must be involved from the beginning in the whole of matter and in every knot, formation and particle of matter; life, mind and whatever is above mind must be latent inactive or concealed active powers in all the operations of material energy."

"We have to come back to the idea of a spirit present in the universe and, if the process of its works of power and its appearance is in the steps of an evolution, there imposes itself the necessity of a previous involution."

Sri Aurobindo, *Rebirth and Karma*, Section I, Chapter 7, Involution and Evolution, pp. 59-60

The Greater and Greater Births of the Spirit

The progressive evolution of physical forms provides a foundation for the higher powers of consciousness to manifest. These powers, as they manifest, then begin to modify and adjust the lower basis to more effectively, finely and precisely respond to the needs of that higher force of consciousness.

Sri Aurobindo takes us through a review of the stages that we can thus far see and identify: "Life takes hold of matter and breathes into it the numberless figures of its abundant creative force, its subtle and variable patterns, its enthusiasm of birth and death and growth and act and response, its will of more and more complex organisation of experience, its quivering search and feeling out after a self-consciousness of its own pleasure and pain and understanding gust of action; mind seizes on life to make it an instrument for the wonders of will and intelligence; soul possesses and lifts mind through the attraction of beauty and good and wisdom and greatness towards the joy of some half-seen ideal highest existence; and in all this miraculous movement and these climbing greatnesses each step sets its foot on a higher rung and opens to a clearer, larger and fuller scope and view of the always secret and always self-manifesting spirit in things."

We see in the increasingly complex and responsive physical evolution an outward sign and indicator of the increasing action of the higher levels of consciousness, but do not yet see the inner meaning of this development until we ourselves move sufficiently up the ladder of consciousness to get an overview. "...the evolution of life opening to mind, the evolution of mind opening to the soul of its own light and action, the evolution of soul out of the limited powers of mind to a resplendent blaze of the infinities of spiritual being are the more significant things, give us greater and subtler reaches of the self-disclosing Secrecy. The physical evolution is only an outward sign, the more and more complex and subtle development of a supporting structure, the growing exterior metre mould of form which is devised to sustain in matter the rising intonations of the spiritual harmony."

"Life itself is only a coloured vehicle, physical birth a convenience for the greater and greater births of the Spirit."

Sri Aurobindo, *Rebirth and Karma*, Section I, Chapter 7, Involution and Evolution, pp. 60-61

Involution and Evolution Provide the Key to the Manifestation of Consciousness in the Universe

Sri Aurobindo describes a concept developed in the Upanishads: "The Upanishad in a telling figure applies the image of the spider which brings its web out of itself and creates the structure in which it takes its station. That is applied in the ancient Scripture not to the evolution of things out of Matter, but to an original bringing of temporal becoming out of the eternal infinity; Matter itself and this material universe are only such a web or indeed no more than a part of it brought out from the spiritual being of the Infinite."

The idea here is that the manifestation is something that takes place out of the substance of the original Consciousness. All of the forms that eventually manifest are contained inherent within the universal Being and Consciousness. Sri Aurobindo explains in more detail: "A Force inherent in the Infinite brings out of it eternally the structure of its action in a universe of which the last descending scale is based upon an involution of all the powers of the spirit into an inconscient absorption in her self-oblivious passion of form and structural working." This is analogous to the tree packing and involving into the seed all the Force and capacity to later create a new formation of that tree.

As with the seed, with all the latent power of the tree contained within it, Matter holds latent within it the involved Force of all the levels of the manifestation, to systematically develop and evolve as the conditions for that development are presented through the process of Time. Sri Aurobindo explains it: "Thence comes an ascent and progressive liberation of power after power till the spirit self-disclosed and set free by knowledge and mastery of its works repossesses the eternal fullness of its being which envelops then and carries in its grasp the manifold and unified splendours of its nature."

Through this process, first of involution of consciousness, and later of evolution of those powers of consciousness through Time, we see the life-process of the universal Being. "Our world-action figures an evolution, an outrolling of a manifold Power gathered and coiled up in the crude intricacy of Matter. The upward progress of the successive births of things is a rise into waking and larger and larger light of a consciousness shut into the first hermetic cell of sleep of the eternal Energy."

Sri Aurobindo, *Rebirth and Karma*, Section I, Chapter 7, Involution and Evolution, pg.61

Ascending the Ladder of Consciousness From Matter To Spirit

Sri Aurobindo describes an interesting corollary between the involution and evolution of Consciousness in the universe, and the process that one undergoes internally in the development of consciousness as described by Kundalini Yoga. Essentially this internal process mirrors the universal process.

"There is a parallel in the Yogic experience of the Kundalini, eternal Force coiled up in the bottom root vessel or chamber, *muladhara*, pedestal, earth-centre of the physical nervous system. There she slumbers coiled up there like a Python and filled full of all that she holds gathered in her being, but when she is struck by the freely coursing breath, by the current of Life which enters in to search for her, she awakes and rises flaming up the ladder of the spinal chord and forces open centre after centre of the involved dynamic secrets of consciousness till at the summit she finds, joins and becomes one with the spirit."

The powers of consciousness are "involved" in Matter, represented by the root chakra, and as they begin to evolve, they open up ever higher centres of energy, known as "chakras". Each chakra represents another rung on the ladder of consciousness, the "life-energy" centers, the higher "life-energy" centers (such as emotions), the basic mental powers, the higher mental powers, the spiritual capacities which unfold as the crown chakra is reached and the energy involved therein is manifested.

"At the highest summit she rises into the self-knowledge of the spirit which informed her action, but because of its involution or concealment in the forms of its workings could not be known in the greatness of its reality. Spirit and Nature discovering the secret of her energies become one at the top of the spiritual evolution by a soul in Nature which awakens to the significance of its own being in the liberation of the highest truth: it comes to know that its births were the births, the assumptions of form of an eternal Spirit, to know itself as that and not a creature of Nature and rises to the possession of the revealed, full and highest power of its own real and spiritual nature. That liberation, because liberation is self-possession, comes to us as the crown of a spiritual evolution."

Sri Aurobindo, *Rebirth and Karma*, Section I, Chapter 7, Involution and Evolution, pg.61-62

Matter Is a Form of Spirit

The deeper modern science goes in exploring Matter, the closer it comes to an understanding that there is a spiritual self-conscious being that manifests itself in the universe, and that Matter is a form of Spirit. First, the scientists recognized that Matter is Energy. Then further research yielded the understanding that Energy is Consciousness. When we look at modern physics, quantum theory, string theory and other cutting-edge theories, we find scientists now recognizing more and more clearly the intentionality and the consciousness implicit in the world of Matter. Matter is not dead, inanimate and simply dense "stuff". It is actually alive with energy; in fact, so much energy that releasing it can create enormous power as we see in atom bombs and nuclear power plants!

What is missing when we see Matter as "inanimate" is simply that we do not have the ability to see and understand the packed intensity and density of Matter. Just as we now recognize an electro-magnetic spectrum that includes waves that are both above and below our threshold of perception, there are expressions of energy and consciousness both above and below our ability to perceive them.

Sri Aurobindo described the relationship of Matter to Life, Mind and Spirit as follows: "Material energy would be then Life packed into the density of Matter and feeling out in it for its own intenser recognisable power which it finds within itself in the material concealment and liberates into action. Life itself would be an energy of a secret mind, a mind imprisoned in its own forms and quivering out in the nervous seekings of life for its intenser recognisable power of consciousness which it discovers within the vital and material suppression and liberates into sensibility....Mind too might only be an inferior scale and formulation derived from a much greater and supramental consciousness, and that consciousness too with its greater light and will a characteristic originating power of spiritual being, the power which secret in all things, in mind, in life, in matter, in the plant and the metal and the atom assures constantly by its inevitable action the idea and harmony of the universe."

"Therefore all things here are expression, form, energy, action of the Spirit; matter itself is but form of spirit, life but power of being of the spirit, mind but working of consciousness of the spirit. All Nature is a display and a play of God, power and action and self-creation of the one spiritual Being."

Sri Aurobindo, *Rebirth and Karma*, Section I, Chapter 7, Involution and Evolution, pp. 62-64

The Evolution of the Spirit in Human Existence

When we look at the involution of Spirit into Matter, and the subsequent evolution of Consciousness in successive stages out of Matter to realize the spiritual consciousness in material forms, we find that the role of the soul in this activity can be more clearly understood and defined. The soul is an individual formation of the One Universal Being and as such it acts as the lynch-pin or bridge between the evolution of material forms and the spiritual consciousness. The soul is able to increase its awareness and self-expression as it moves through the various levels of creation that represent the increasing power of consciousness evolving out of Matter.

Sri Aurobindo discusses the role of the soul within the framework of our human birth: "Our humanity is the conscious meeting place of the finite and the infinite and to grow more and more towards that Infinite even in this physical birth is our privilege. This Infinite, this Spirit who is housed within us but not bound or shut in by mind or body, is our own self and to find and be our self was, as the ancient sages knew, always the object of our human striving, for it is the object of the whole immense working of Nature."

For the most part humans are immersed in the subconscient or subliminal parts of the being until we grow beyond the limits of the mind, life and body and enter realms of superconscient awareness. "When he becomes conscient in the superconscience, the heights and depths of his being will be illumined by another light of knowledge than the flickering lamp of the reason can now cast into a few corners; for then the master of the field will enlighten this whole wonderful field of his being, as the sun illumines the whole system it has created out of its glories. Then only he can know the reality even of his own mind and life and body."

This change of consciousness brings about a transformation of the human existence: "Mind will be changed into a greater consciousness, his life will be a direct power and action of the Divinity, his very body no longer this first gross lump of breathing clay, but a very image and body of spiritual being. That transfiguration on the summit of the mountain, divine birth, *divya janma*, is that to which all these births are a long series of laborious steps. An involution of spirit in matter is the beginning, but a spiritual assumption of divine birth is the fullness of the evolution."

Sri Aurobindo, *Rebirth and Karma*, Section I, Chapter 7, Involution and Evolution, pp.64-65

East Meets West

It is a common observation that the focus of the West and the focus of the East diverge and are opposed to one another. The West has developed a society based on incredible concentration on the organization and enhancement of the vital force of life in the material sphere. The East meanwhile is noted for its attention on the life of the Spirit, with its signature achievement being the abandonment of the things of this world for the spiritual realization.

Each of these two directions, however, gains support and significance through the perfection of both sides of the equation. They are complementary directions rather than opposites.

The Truth of the spiritual principle encompasses both the transcendent Beyond, and the manifest universe, which is the carrying out into form of the Spirit. Matter, Life and Mind are all principles of spiritual action and when properly understood, must obtain their sustenance from the Spirit. At the same time a concentration solely on the material sphere, without recognition of the spiritual principles that are the source and meaning of the manifestation, is doomed to transitory results and ends in vain material aggrandizement.

Sri Aurobindo brings the two together as complementary and, indeed, aspects of the same Truth: "The truths of universal existence are of two kinds, truths of the spirit which are themselves eternal and immutable, and these are the great things that cast themselves out into becoming and there constantly realise their powers and significances, and the play of the consciousness with them, the discords, the musical variations, soundings of possibility, progressive notations, reversions, perversions, mounting conversions into a greater figure of harmony; and of all these things the spirit has made, makes always his universe. But it is himself that he makes in it, himself that is the creator and the energy of creation and the cause and the method and the result of the working, the mechanist and the machine, the music and the musician, the poet and the poem, supermind, mind and life and matter, the soul and Nature."

Sri Aurobindo, *Rebirth and Karma*, Section I, Chapter 7, Involution and Evolution, pg. 65

The Unity of Soul and Nature

It is the nature of the mental consciousness to tend to divide and fragment, and it does this through "exclusive concentration" on one aspect at the expense of the others that make up the unified whole that is our existence. Thus, the mind treats soul as something opposed to nature, just as it treats spirit as something opposed to matter. Sri Aurobindo does not accept these artificial oppositions however: ""But Soul and Nature, Purusha and Prakriti, are two eternal lovers who possess their perpetual unity and enjoy their constant difference, and in the unity abound in the passion of the multitudinous play of their difference, and in every step of the difference abound in the secret sense or the overt consciousness of unity."

The soul is involved in Nature, apparently asleep, but nevertheless there. This is the process in the subconscient realms of Matter and Life. There is a corresponding process at the superconscient levels of conscious awareness, where Nature is involved in the "trance of oneness with the absorbed self-possession of the spirit."

The resolution of the apparent contradiction comes about: "The soul fulfils itself in Nature when it possesses in her the consciousness of that eternity and its power and joy and transfigures the natural becoming with the fullness of the spiritual being. The constant self-creation which we call birth finds there the perfect evolution of all that it held in its own nature and reveals its own utmost significance. The complete soul possesses all its self and all Nature."

Sri Aurobindo, *Rebirth and Karma*, Section I, Chapter 7, Involution and Evolution, pp. 65-66

Evolution and the Meaning of Life

Sri Aurobindo summarizes the discussion about involution and evolution with the following: "Therefore all this evolution is a growing of the Self in material nature to the conscious possession of its own spiritual being."

The material forms that we see around us are not dead or inanimate, but are rather densely packed forms of energy, organized in such a way as to hold tremendous power and consciousness within the apparent immobility. The consciousness that creates the universe is thus involved in these material forms, and they become the basis for the evolution, the systematic unfolding of the powers of existence and consciousness held tightly within the forms of matter.

At the end of the evolutionary process we find: "the spirit holding Nature conscious in himself, complete by his completeness, liberated by his liberation, perfected in his perfection, crowns the evolution."

This makes the process of birth and death part of a larger cycle of systematic unfolding of this consciousness of the spirit taking birth as a conscious form in Matter. "To grow in knowledge, in power, in delight, love and oneness, towards the infinite light, capacity and bliss of spiritual existence, to universalise ourselves till we are one with all being, and to exceed constantly our present limited self till it opens fully to the transcendence in which the universal lives and to base upon it all our becoming, that is the full evolution of what now lies darkly wrapped or works half evolved in Nature."

Sri Aurobindo, *Rebirth and Karma*, Section I, Chapter 7, Involution and Evolution, pp. 66-67

CHAPTER EIGHT

KARMA

Introduction To the Concept of Karma

Regardless of background, religion, philosophy, social position or experience, one thing that people intuitively grasp and almost universally accept is that there is some type of universal law that applies to our actions. We may call it "cause and effect", or we may call it "consequences" or we may call it "eternal law", "divine retribution", "judgment day", "damnation" or "law of Nature". In the East, it is called "karma", and it is a tribute to this concept that the word "karma" has found its way easily into the English language and even into daily use. A new website even calls itself "credit karma" and offers to show individuals what their credit worthiness ranking is and provide ways to improve it.

It is true that concepts that are adopted by popular approval tend to become caricatures of the Truth, and so it may be with the popular notions of Karma (under whatever banner or name it is being considered). There is no doubt that some of the ideas that people carry around with this concept do not bear serious scrutiny; however, the core truth contained within is still something that cannot be denied.

Sri Aurobindo points out: "There is a solidity at once of philosophic and of practical truth supporting the idea, a bedrock of the deepest universal undeniable verities against which the human mind must always come up in its fathomings of the fathomless; in this way indeed does the world deal with us, there is a law here which does so make itself felt and against whicha ll our egoistic ignorance and self-will and violence dashes up in the end, as the old Greek poet said of the haughty insolence and prosperous pride of man, against the very foundation of the throne of Zeus, the marble feet of Themis, the adamantine bust of Ananke. There is the secret of an eternal factor, the base of the unchanging action of the just and truthful gods…in the self-sufficient and impartial law of Karma."

Sri Aurobindo, *Rebirth and Karma*, Section I, Chapter 8, Karma, pg. 68

The Starting Point For a
Review of the Principles of Karma

As with all human understanding, humanity has approached the law of karma from our own very limited starting point. We try to essentially bring it down to a personal level and create some kind of ethical rulebook around its operation, or else relate the universal forces to us through some kind of inexorable process that appears to function under certain laws or rules, but directly interacts with our own lives and the decisions we make and the actions we take.

The Buddhist enunciation of the universal law of karma was clearly a breakthrough in terms of treating it as a universal action. In the West, the widening understanding of the vast scope and intelligent activity of the universe has systematically broadened our appreciation for the action of the Forces that are shaping the entire universal action, including, but certainly not limited to our individual lives.

Essentially we are coming to a point in time where we begin to understand that the Creation does not revolve around our own world or our own individuality, and that while we have our role to play, and our own unique value, it is with much larger frameworks and universal laws that we have to grapple to truly begin to understand. Thus, the law of karma includes our own actions, but not as some kind of directed ethical or moral reward or retribution, but as an instance of the universal laws of action, the patterns of energy.

This turns into a much less simplistic model than most of us have entertained to date, and Sri Aurobindo takes up the question with the view toward systematically reviewing it from all angles and aspects to provide a comprehensive basis for understanding. Because we tend to look at things first from the basis of the material world and material energy, we may want to start this review at the point where our vision naturally first engages the issue:

"It may be as well then to start from the physical base in approaching this question of Karma, though we may find at last that it is from the other end of being, from its spiritual summit rather than its material support that we must look in order to catch its whole significance–and to fix also the limits of its significance."

Sri Aurobindo, *Rebirth and Karma*, Section I, Chapter 8, Karma, pp. 68-69

The Universal Law of Cause and Effect

Scientists have developed what they call "laws" of physics. These laws of physics describe the action of material energy, the laws of "cause and effect" in the physical universe. Similarly, we find other applications of the action of cause and effect. We observe that what occurs today is the result of energy expended and directed yesterday; and similarly, today's action creates tomorrow's result. The entire system of life in Western civilisation is based on the principles of cause and effect development.

Sri Aurobindo makes it clear that this action of "cause and effect" is the fundamental essence of what is known in the East as the "law of Karma". "Fundamentally, the meaning of Karma is that all existence is the working of a universal Energy, a process and an action and a building of things by that action,–an unbuilding too, but as a step to farther building,–that all is a continuous chain in which every one link is bound indissolubly to the past infinity of numberless links, and the whole governed by fixed relations, by a fixed association of cause and effect, present action the result of past action as future action will be the result of present action, all cause a working of energy and all effect too a working of energy."

This action works not just on the physical plane, but at all levels of Energy, vital, emotional, mental and spiritual. We can see that by the nature of the energy put forth, a commensurate effect is created.

Sri Aurobindo describes two errors that have crept into the general understanding of the workings of this law of karma and it is useful to review them so that we may, hopefully, counteract them and come to a clearer basis for our understanding: "first, the strenuous paradoxical attempt....to explain supraphysical things by a physical formula, and a darkening second error of setting behind the universal rule of law and as its cause and efficient the quite opposite idea of the cosmic reign of Chance."

Sri Aurobindo makes it clear that in a universe that functions under the kind of strict laws that we see everywhere at work, the idea that it is developed by Chance is incomprehensible. The reason for this mistake is contained as a seed in the first error, in that we attempt to explain things of a different order by an understanding based in the physical world, whereas our expanding insight is now beginning to show us that we need other forms of knowledge and other tools of perception when we begin to explore realms beyond the purely physical world.

Sri Aurobindo, *Rebirth and Karma*, Section I, Chapter 8, Karma, pp. 69-70

Different Forms of Energy
Yield Different Operations of Karma

We recognize that Energy is One. There is a unified continuum within which all energy moves. At the same time, there is a different application of energy depending on the plane on which it is operative and the field upon which it is working. We can see this easily with regard to the electro-magnetic spectrum where we see light waves, sound waves, electricity, magnetism, gravity all operating but having different actions and applications.

Similarly, the law of karma is universal, but it too varies its action to the plane upon which it is working out. Thus, we cannot attribute the results of mental acts to physical causes. It is true that there are influences between different planes which may impact or modify the pure action of a force that would otherwise be able to manifest in all its purity if it were not part of the complex interaction of planes that make up our existence. Thus, we can recognize that a mental act undertaken purely in the mental sphere will yield a potentially somewhat different result than a similar mental act occurring in a world of physical and vital action with those other forces weighing on the mental result.

At the same time, we need to then recognize that karmic response, cause and effect, is tailored to the type of energy put into action and the plane upon which it is operative. Thus, a mental force will have a primarily mental effect; a moral force a primarily moral effect, a physical force a primary physical effect. This actually helps us begin to understand why, for instance, morally "good" actions do not always result in physical or vital benefits–in other words, morally good people do not always get rich or avoid physical suffering, for example.

Sri Aurobindo concludes: "Forms of one universal Force at bottom–or at top–these may be, but in practice they are different energies and have to be so dealt with–until we can find what that universal Force may be in its highest purest texture and initial power and whether that discovery can give us in the perplexities of our nature a unifying direction."

Sri Aurobindo, *Rebirth and Karma*, Section I, Chapter 8, Karma, pp. 70-71

No Chance!

There are those who hold that the entire existence of the universe, and the apparent intelligence we see within the quantum world of sub-atomic energy, as well as in the interactive relationship of all forms of life existence to create an inter-dependent existence, is purely the work of Chance, a random combination of chemical reactions that yielded the "miracle" of Life.

There are those who would continue this line of understanding to make it a matter of "luck" as to how our lives unfold and whether we are "successful" or "failures" in our actions.

This line of approach is essentially at the other end of the continuum from those who take the opposing viewpoint that everything, down to the smallest detail, is absolutely pre-destined and controlled with no amount of random chance whatsoever.

Sri Aurobindo takes issue with the idea that intelligence and consciousness can arise as a result of random chance. "Chance does not at all exist; it is only a word by which we cover and excuse our own ignorance. Science excludes it from the actual process of physical law; everything there is determined by fixed cause and relation. But when it comes to ask why these relations exist and not others, why a particular cause is allied to a particular effect, it finds that it knows nothing whatever about the matter; every actualised possibility supposes a number of other possibilities that have not actualised but conceivably might have, and it is convenient then to say that Chance or at most a dominant probability determines all actual happening, the chance of evolution, the stumblings of a groping inconscient energy which somehow finds out some good enough way and fixes itself into a repetition of the process."

Sri Aurobindo's view of the universe starts from a universal Consciousness that creates forms and energies out of itself, first through a process of involution, and then through a process of evolution. Inherent at all times is that universal consciousness and being. The inter-relationships and fine detail of the mechanisms and processes, the inter-dependencies and symbiotic relations all point to an incredibly complex consciousness that embraces the whole, at both the macro-and micro-levels. This is not the result of Chance!

Sri Aurobindo, *Rebirth and Karma*, Section I, Chapter 8, Karma, pg. 71

The Need For a Moral and Spiritual Law of Being

Scientists have gained an increasing level of understanding of the laws of Matter. The development of Quantum Mechanics has led to a much more subtle view of the intelligence and energy within the material world. However, when science approaches the motive springs which shape our actions as human beings, including our moral, ethical and spiritual impulses, there remains an enormous gap in knowledge. The explanations based on material causes fall far short, and the theories which arise to try to fill in the lack of knowledge are weak and incomplete.

The moral, ethical and spiritual principles originate on a different plane than material substance, and thus, we must be able to eventually identify with and understand the native level of action of the energies operative on these other planes, in order to create a clear sense of the laws that are operative there.

The real dilemma and struggle that we face as human beings revolves far more around the significance of our existence, and our moral and spiritual seeking, than it does around the physical principles that govern the material world within which we live. Sri Aurobindo makes clear the need, therefore, to develop a deeper insight and understanding of the higher laws of our being: "To know the law of my moral and spiritual being is at first and last more imperative for me than to learn the ways of steam and electricity, for without these outward advantages I can grow in my inner manhood, but not without some notion of moral and spiritual law. Action is demanded of me and I need a rule for my action: something I am urged inwardly to become which I am not yet, and I would know what is the way and law, what the central power or many conflicting powers and what the height and possible range and perfection of my becoming. That surely much more than the rule of electrons or the possibilities of a more omnipotent physical machinery and more powerful explosives is the real human question."

Sri Aurobindo, *Rebirth and Karma*, Section I, Chapter 8, Karma, pp. 71-72

Buddhism and the Law of Karma

Physical scientists focus on and describe the laws that govern the operations of matter and energy on the material plane. They are unable, however, to provide us any realistic insight to the operation of moral and ethical laws for our higher emotional and mental parts of our being. Buddhism however takes up this challenge and proposes a schema of law and organized action for the moral being of man, through their discussion of the law of karma. The Buddhist framework provides us the system that explains and helps us to gain mastery over our moral and ethical impulses and our relationships to the social organization of life.

At the same time, just as the physical scientists cannot and do not explain anything beyond the physical laws of nature, the Buddhist conception assigns what is beyond our human range to a silent, uninvolved status, called Nirvana, which is beyond the impulsions of the senses and the force of desire, and therefore, is the place where the law of karma is dissolved into a Oneness of quiescence.

Sri Aurobindo, while acknowledging the progress represented by the Buddhist conception, also notes that it has a similar gap when it goes beyond the mental/emotional status of humanity, to what the physical scientist has when he tries to go beyond physical, material nature.

Sri Aurobindo advises that just as the next stage of progress revealed the operations of a set of principles, so also when we move beyond the limitations of the human mental framework, we can expect to find another level and a corresponding set of principles operative there.

"It is by no means so certain that a high spiritual negation of what I am is my only possible road to perfection; a high spiritual affirmation and absolute of what I am may be also a feasible way and gate."

"To the everlasting No the living being may resign itself by an effort, a sorrowful or a superb turning upon itself and existence, but the everlasting Yes is its native attraction: our spiritual orientation, the magnetism that draws the soul, is to eternal Being and not to eternal Non-Being."

Sri Aurobindo, *Rebirth and Karma*, Section I, Chapter 8, Karma, pp. 72-73

The Four Pillars of the Complete Theory of Karma

Having established that there is an organised law of action at the moral and mental levels, as at the physical level, we avoid the issue of everything occurring through chance, and provide an underpinning of intentionality to the universe. It is easy, however, at this point to go to the opposite extreme and assert that everything is in fact pre-determined and that there is thus no free will, but only the illusion of free will. The debate about predestination and free will has occupied human beings for our entire existence in one way or another.

Sri Aurobindo sets forth at this point the 4 steps in the law of karma which help us to avoid both extremes and come to a balanced view of the role of karma in the unfolding of the universe. The first step is the existence of the law of karma in and of itself on the planes of mental and moral energy. The second step is the "Idea which creates all relations." The concept of a formative Idea has played an important role as well, with the Bible's assertion "In the beginning was the Word" being just one example, while the concepts of Plato, and Goethe have a similar causative role for the Idea. Sri Aurobindo, in another place, implied this when he indicated that the French Revolution took place because of a yogi in a cave in the Himalayan mountains dreaming of freedom. Once again, if we go to the extreme here and attribute ultimate reality to the Idea with nothing further, then we lose any independent existence for ourselves.

Thus enters the third "pillar": "I am a soul developing and persisting in the paths of the universal Energy and that in myself is the seed of all my creation. What I have become, I have made myself by the soul's past idea and action, its inner and outer karma; what I will to be, I can make myself by present and future idea and action." The acknowledgement of the reality and role of the soul provides the opportunity for the exercise of free will within the larger scope and context of the action of the Idea under the impulsion of the universal Laws.

The fourth pillar then: "...there is this last supreme liberating step that both the Idea and its Karma may have their origin in the free spirit and by arriving at myself by experience and self-finding I can exalt my state beyond all bondage of Karma to spiritual freedom. These are the four pillars of the complete theory of Karma. They are also the four truths of the dealings of Self with Nature."

Sri Aurobindo, *Rebirth and Karma*, Section I, Chapter 8, Karma, pp. 73-74

CHAPTER NINE

KARMA AND FREEDOM

Reconciling Opposites

The mental consciousness which is generally predominant for human beings, tends to see things as distinct and separate and it thereby creates what are known as a play of "opposites" that are in conflict with one another. Whether it is the battle of the forces of Light and Darkness as described in some of the ancient religions, or the opposition of God and the Devil, Good and Evil, Right and Wrong, we find these distinctions throughout human history and in virtually all religious and philosophical traditions.

At the same time, we expect that one will "triumph" over the other and we develop concepts that imply that good can exist without evil, or that darkness may be banished forever. Others recognize that these pairs of opposites are somehow inextricably intertwined with one another and take the position that we can never have one without the other.

Some have recognized that what appears to us to be "evil" in many cases eventually yields "good"; and on the contrary, what is considered "good" may yield evil. The Chinese symbology of the yin/yang implies that light and dark are part of one larger inter-relationship and are contained within one another and move between each other.

One potential solution is to recognize that the opposites are actually complementary aspects or poles of one spectrum, and that another form of solution is possible whereby one transcends and embraces. Sri Aurobindo describes this approach: "And it is said too that on the other side of the human being and beyond its struggles is a serenity of the high and universal spirit where the soul transcends sin, but transcends also virtue, and neither sorrows nor repents nor asks 'Why have I not done the good and wherefore have I done this which is evil?' (Taittiriya Upanishad) because in it all things are perfect and to it all things are pure."

Sri Aurobindo, *Rebirth and Karma*, Section I, Chapter 9, Karma and Freedom, pg. 75

Karma, Free-Will and Necessity

Due to our mental nature that divides everything into convenient oppositions, we eventually look at even our development of consciousness as an opposition between the Knowledge and the Ignorance. This view of things provides us at least with a more basic cause for what we call "good" and "evil" on a more surface level. We can eventually resolve the concept of ignorance into a partially revealed, partially withheld form of knowledge, caused by the involution of consciousness into Matter and the subsequent step-by-step evolutionary process that it undertakes to manifest the consciousness in the forms.

As we begin to reflect on the nature of the energy that we have called "the law of karma" we see that it is a law of "cause and effect". The present circumstances are caused by past event, and in turn create future events. The question next arises as to whether this is a predetermined result and what role there is, if any, for "freedom". We have a more or less "innate" aspiration for freedom and intuitively we believe that we have free-will. While there is no doubt that past impulsion and environmental and social factors make much of what happens more or less inevitable, the essence is whether there is somewhere within our being the capability of extracting ourselves from this driven process and exercising "freedom".

Sri Aurobindo weighs in on this conundrum: "So much of what we are and do is determined by our environment, so much has been shaped by our education and upbringing,–we are made by life and by the hands of others, are clay for many potters: and, as for what is left, was it not determined, even that which is most ourselves, by our individual, our racial, our human heredity or in the last resort by universal Nature who has shaped man and each man to what he is for her blind or her conscient uses?"

It is easy to become trapped in the logic of predestination based on such a review, when the only factor that is obviously in favor of "free will" is our inner certainty, which implies that "free will" must operate at some level beyond or separate from the mental, vital and physical nature that constitutes our normal human instrument of action.

Sri Aurobindo, *Rebirth and Karma*, Section I, Chapter 9, Karma and Freedom, pg. 75-76

Is There Such a Thing As Free Will?

The ongoing debate about free will versus determinism frames much of human history. We instinctively feel like we have free choice and can determine our own destiny, overcoming genetics, upbringing, and societal limitations to achieve success in our lives, and change who and what we are, and what we become. To some degree, however, this "instinct" is similar to our erroneous perception that the sun revolves around the earth rather than the other way around! If we look deeply at the question of free will, we can see various lines of impulsion which have conditioned and in most cases determined our "free" choice. In fact, modern day social scientists, such as Nobel Prize winning author Daniel Kahneman in his recent book *Thinking, Fast and Slow* has illustrated numerous instances where our "free choice" is conditioned by training, language, background and various propensities.

Sri Aurobindo discusses this issue as follows: "But this will and its effort, is it not itself an instrument, even a mechanical engine of Nature, the active universal energy, and is not its freedom an arbitrary illusion of our mentality which lives in each moment of the present and separates it by ignorance, by an abstraction of the mind from its determining past, so that I seem at every critical moment to exercise a free and virgin choice, while all the time my choice is dominated by its own previous formation and by all that obscure past which I ignore?"

In order to adopt the idea of free will, it becomes necessary to find some part of our existence or being which stands outside of and independent from the action of Nature. "Only if there is a soul or self which is not a creation, but a master of Nature, not a formation of the stream of universal energy, but itself the former and creator of its own Karma, are we justified in our claim of an actual freedom or at least in our aspiration to a real liberty."

Sri Aurobindo, *Rebirth and Karma*, Section I, Chapter 9, Karma and Freedom, pp. 76-77

Freedom From Karma?

Once we recognize the chain of karma and our subservience to it, we begin to consider whether it is possible to ever free ourselves from this chain of causality. Are we forever bound to run on this treadmill? Is there no way to change this relationship, either by getting off the treadmill, or finding a standpoint outside of it?

It is an axiom of modern social science that we are always defined by the frame within which we experience our lives, and that we cannot see that frame; however, once we step outside of that frame, one way or another, we can look in with a new perspective and a new freedom.

The brilliance of the Buddhist approach was to essentially recognize this truth and understand that the way out is to be liberated through dissolution of the motive power of the karmic bond. Sri Aurobindo describes it in this way: "The motive power which keeps Karma in motion is desire and attachment to its works, and by the conviction of impermanence and the cessation of desire there can come about an extinction of the continuity of the idea in the succession of Time."

The solution therefore is what one may call a "negative" state of dissolution, inaction, removal from the chain. The Buddhist approach does not provide a positive freedom of the soul, because it does not recognize the need or existence of the soul.

The Mayavadin approach recognizes the soul's existence, but it too is focused on "liberation" in its essentially negative sense of non-action, non-attachment. It is however the recognition of a Self, a Soul, which provides us a basis for a further development, a positive freedom that can possess and master the law of Karma.

"What we see in both these systems is that spiritual freedom and the cosmic compulsion are equally admitted, but in a total separation and an exclusion from each other's own proper field,–still as absolute opposites and contraries. Compulsion of ignorance or Karma is absolute in the world of birth; freedom of the spirit is absolute in a withdrawal from birth and cosmos and Karma."

We can see by the focus on opposition and exclusion that we are still operating within the framework of the mental power, the power that divides, fragments, separates and divides.

Sri Aurobindo, *Rebirth and Karma*, Section I, Chapter 9, Karma and Freedom, pp. 77-78

Are Karma and Freedom Incompatible?

Sri Aurobindo's approach is consistent in that he always seeks for the larger synthesis that reconciles apparently irreconcilable opposites into complementary poles or aspects of one continuum. He is able to provide us a clue to the reconciliation of karma and freedom: "Buddhism and Illusionism too do not assert any external or internal predestination, but only a self-imposed bondage. And very insistently they demand of man a choice between the right and the wrong way, between the will to an impermanent existence and the will to Nirvana, between a will to cosmic existence and the will to an absolute spiritual being. Nor do they demand this choice of the Absolute or of the universal Being and Power, who indeed cares nothing for their claim and goes on very tranquilly and securely with his mighty eternal action, but they ask it of the individual, of the soul of man halting perplexed between the oppositions of his mentality. It would seem then that there is something in our individual being which has some real freedom of will, some power of choice of a great consequence and magnitude, and what is it then that thus chooses, and what are the limits, where the beginning or the end of its actual or its possible liberty?"

Once we acknowledge that there is something within the individual being that can exercise free choice, even if we, for the moment, limit that free choice to participation and non-participation in the cosmic action, we are able to escape the bonds of Karma and the impulsion towards a strict predetermined universal unfolding which would otherwise force itself upon us.

We may also go further, of course, and suppose that if we have the freedom to participate, or not, and are thus able to establish some part of us which is independent of the law of Karma, the chain of cause and effect in action, then it may also be possible to find the standpoint within ourselves where the choice of participation or non-participation itself is no longer restricting our freedom.

In such an instance we would find that "freedom" and "Karma" are actually able to exist side by side, each fulfilling its role and purpose.

Sri Aurobindo, *Rebirth and Karma*, Section I, Chapter 9, Karma and Freedom, pp. 78-79

Finding Freedom of the
Spirit in the World of Forms

If there is a reality to free will it must be placed in a poise or standpoint outside the operations of Karma. The freedom to participate or not in the world of cause and effect, which we have seen as a hallmark of the Buddhist and Illusionist understanding, provided us the clue that there must be some consciousness that exists outside the causal action. We may also find another clue in the extremely complex and subtle inter-working of the world of forms and actions, which clearly cannot have developed by "chance" or as the result of an "illusion". The illusion results, not from the world of forms itself, but through our artificial division and fragmentation of the unified Whole and through our attachment to the things of the world rather than the much wider understanding that links us to the Spirit and the significance of the unfolding universe.

Sri Aurobindo sums this up with the following: "...some secret self-knowledge and wisdom there must be which guides the Energy of Karma in its idea and has appointed for her the paths she must hew in Time. It is because of their persistence of principle in all the transiences of particular form that things have such a hold on our mind and will. It is because the world is so real that we feel so potently its grasp on us and our spirits turn on it with this grip of the wrestler."

Sri Aurobindo's conclusion is that if we seek for liberty it is liberty of the spirit: "We shall do better then to fix on that other more generally admissible distinction, namely, of the world of Karma as a practical or relative reality and the being of the Spirit constant behind it or brooding above it as a greater supreme reality. And then we have to find whether in the latter alone is any touch of freedom or whether, as must surely be if it is the Spirit that presides over the Energy at work and over its action, there is here too some element or some beginning at least of liberty, and whether, even if it be small and quite relative, we cannot in these steps of Time, in these relations of Karma make this freedom great and real by dwelling consciously in the greatness of the Spirit. May not that be the sovereignty we shall find here when we rise to the top of the soul's evolution?"

Sri Aurobindo, *Rebirth and Karma*, Section I, Chapter 9, Karma and Freedom, pp. 79-80

The Mental Consciousness Develops the Sense of Free Will

Even the most careful observation we can make of the physical world fails to show us the action of free will. While an innate and extremely precise and powerful intelligence clearly has developed the material world, everything seems to be acting under very specific laws. There is no room for any kind of innovative and unscripted action in the material field.

With the development of the life energy, as Sri Aurobindo points out, we begin to see some other principles of action emerge. We begin to see options, opportunities and a process of selection which seems to be less bound to inflexible and unchanging laws.

The development of the mental energy provides a further impetus to the concept of free will. "…Nature becomes there much more widely conscious of possibility and of choice; mind is aware of potentialities and of determinations in idea which are other than those of the immediate actuality or of the fixedly necessary consequence of the sum of past and present actualities; it is aware of numberless "may-be's" and "might-have-been's", and these last are not entirely dead rejected things, but can return through the power of the Idea and effect future determinations and can fulfil themselves at last in the inner reality of their idea though, it may well be, in other forms and circumstances. Moreover, mind can and does go still further; it can conceive of an infinite possibility behind the self-limitations of actual existence. And from this seeing there arises the idea of a free and infinite Will, a Will of illimitable potentiality which determines all these innumerable marvels of its own universal becoming or creation in Space and Time. That means the absolute freedom of a Spirit and Power which is not determined by Karma. Apparent Necessity is the child of the spirit's free self-determination. What affects us as Necessity, is a Will which works in sequence and not a blind Force driven by its own mechanism."

This essential response of the mind to the opportunities for development is not necessarily a solution to the question of free will versus a larger determinism, but it provides us with the sense of intuition that may represent the working of a greater Truth beyond the limits that the mind can effectively grasp, and provides us substance for our further review in this direction.

Sri Aurobindo, *Rebirth and Karma*, Section I, Chapter 9, Karma and Freedom, pp. 80-81

Three Conceptions of the Nature of Existence

While there are many ideas about the nature of existence, there are three that seem to capture the primary directions, albeit with variances based on viewpoints of different perspectives. These three include an essential non-theistic approach of some kind of mechanical universal Necessity; a theistic approach of an infinite Being, a Creator who has essentially created and developed the universal manifestation, and then there is the concept of an Existence which develops the relations of the universe, populates it with aspects of itself in the form of souls, and allows their free interaction within the framework of the basic principles of existence.

Sri Aurobindo describes the nature of the first conception: "The nature of this Necessity would be that of a fixed processus bound to certain initial and general determinations of which all the rest is the consequence." "...against or behind that nothing or some absolute non-existence." This conception obviously does not explain very much, but responds to our physical sense of the world around us without delving deeper beyond the surface appearance.

The concept of an external Creator is of course extremely widely disseminated, particularly in the West. Sri Aurobindo describes this concept in the bigger picture of reviewing the nature of existence: "Then, there is the idea of a free infinite Being, God or Absolute, who somehow or other creates out of something or out of nothing, in reality or only in conception, or brings out of himself into manifestation a world of the necessity of his will or Maya or Karma in which all things, all creatures are bound as the victims of a necessity, not mechanical or external, but spiritual and internal, a force of Ignorance or a force of Karma or else some kind of arbitrary predestination." While this conception moves beyond the limits of a purely external mechanical universe, it does not yet imply any operation of free will in the universe.

The third conception is described as follows: "And, finally, there is the idea of an absolute free Existence which supports, develops and informs a universe of relations, of that Power as the universal Spirit of our existence, of the world as the evolution of these relations, of beings in the universe as souls who work them out with some freedom of the spirit as the basis,–for that they inwardly are,–but with an observation of the law of the relations as their natural condition."

It is in this third approach that we see the possibility of free will entering into the relations of the universe.

Sri Aurobindo, *Rebirth and Karma*, Section I, Chapter 9, Karma and Freedom, pg. 81

Free in the Spirit, Subject to the Law of Nature in Action

When we review the 3 concepts of the nature of existence, it becomes clear that the first two have been widely explored in the past and leave us unsatisfied due to the apparent weaknesses in their positions. The third one, the free and eternal Spirit manifesting through individual souls within the framework of the action of Nature, and becoming ever more conscious as higher stages of evolution manifest, clearly requires a further review and deeper consideration.

In this instance, the fact that the law of Nature is being carried out and allowed to operate does not negate the inner or underlying freedom of the Spirit. Since the Spirit created this process, it is certainly reasonable to expect that it would abide by that process in its systematic evolution of consciousness in the manifestation. It is analogous to a business organisation setting up a series of procedures and having everyone in the organisation, including the founders and top management personnel, work within that framework. The decision is one of "choice", but there is a benefit to working within the framework that has been developed.

Sri Aurobindo comments on this concept: "This law would be in phenomenon or as seen in a superficial view of its sole outward machinery an apparent chain of necessity, but in fact it would be a free self-determination of the Spirit in existence. The free self and spirit would be there informing all the action of material energy, secretly conscient in its inconscience; his would be the movement of life and its inner spirit of guidance; but in mind would be something of the first open light of his presence."

The progressive development of new and higher powers of consciousness, unfolding successively through Matter, Life and Mind, would appear to be totally involved and bound at the material level, still bound but gaining a sense of more free action in Life and, while still bound in Mind, awakening to the higher possibilities of freedom by contact with the higher spiritual powers of creation.

This would yield a result "Free in the spirit within, conditioned and determined in Nature, striving in his soul to bring out the spiritual light, mastery and freedom to work upon the obscurity and embarrassment of his first natural conditions and their narrow determinations, this would be the nature of man the mental being."

Sri Aurobindo, *Rebirth and Karma*, Section I, Chapter 9, Karma and Freedom, pp. 81-82

The Free Individual Power of the Spirit Uses Karma As Its Instrument of Action

As long as we place ourselves within the framework of Body, Life and Mind, and identify ourselves with them, we have the perception that we are bound by the chain of cause and effect, the law of Karma. In order to escape from this bondage, the most frequently proposed solutions involve abandonment of the force of desire, and the consequent abandonment of the life and actions of the world. Whether this leads to "nirvana" or to an absolute, silent and unmoving identification with the eternal Brahman, the path is away from the world.

Sri Aurobindo proposes another solution, however. This solution assigns a real significance and purpose to the life in the world and the evolution of consciousness that we see as the defining thread running through the development we can observe or infer. He accepts the idea that the law of Karma is the instrument of this development. The idea of freedom from karma, which in the past has been based on abandonment of the life of action, needs to find a new meaning from this viewpoint.

Sri Aurobindo finds the answer to this conundrum in the idea that the eternal Spirit, which stands outside the action of Nature, and shapes, controls and utilizes it, has an element here within the framework, but nevertheless independent of it and partaking of the freedom of the Spirit. This is the individual soul. The mind, life and body, as instruments of Nature, are subject to the law of Karma.

Sri Aurobindo explains: "These things are subject to the action of Karma, but man in himself, the real man within is not its subject, *na karma lipyate nare*". Rather is Karma his instrument and its developments the material he uses, and he is using it always from life to life for the shaping of a limited and individual, which may be one day a divine and cosmic personality. For the eternal spirit enjoys an absolute freedom."

The Spirit is free, both outside the manifestation and within it. The action, the energy, the materiality does not bind the freedom of the Spirit. To the extent that we recognize that the individual soul partakes of the eternal Spirit, it too must be free.

"But if….there is any such thing as an individual power of spirit, it must, in whatever degree of actuality share in the united force and freedom of the self-existent Divinity; for it is being of his being."

Sri Aurobindo, *Rebirth and Karma*, Section I, Chapter 9, Karma and Freedom, pp. 82-83

Partial Freedom
Constrained By the Law of Karma

Our identification with the Mind, Life and Body, through the device of the ego-personality, ensures that we experience the limitations caused by the law of Karma. This is to some degree a protective device while consciousness systematically unfolds and manifests to ever greater extents in the world. Just as we stake a young tree to protect it from the wind, the law of Karma acts as a guiding factor while we act predominantly from the basis of Ignorance due to the deeply involved nature of Consciousness in the material world. Until we are ready for freedom, we are aided by the cause-effect nature of action in the world, and we thereby are able to test our understanding and fine tune our line of action, as we systematically learn and grow into a greater consciousness, and with it, a greater freedom.

Sri Aurobindo reviews the reason for this: "I appear to be bound by the law of an outward and imposed energy only because there is separation between my outward nature and my inmost spiritual self and I do not live in that outwardness with my whole being, but with a shape, turn and mental formation of myself which I call my ego or my personality."

Since Mind also partakes of the nature of Ignorance, it cannot also act with untrammeled freedom: "An Ignorance cannot be permitted to have, even if in its nature it could have, free mastery. It would never do for an ignorant mind and will to be given a wide and real freedom; for it would upset the right order of the energy which the Spirit has set at work and produce a most unholy confusion. It must be forced to obey or, if it resists, to bear the reaction of the Law; its partial freedom of a clouded and stumbling knowledge must be constantly overruled both in its action and its result by the law of universal Nature and the will of the seeing universal Spirit who governs the dispositions and consequences of Karma. This constrained overruled action is in patent fact the character of our mental being and action."

Sri Aurobindo, *Rebirth and Karma*, Section I, Chapter 9, Karma and Freedom, pp. 83-84

Freedom Is Of the Soul,
Not the Surface Personality

There remains within each of us a sense that we have "free will". Close examination shows us that the actions of body, life and mind are conditioned by past causes. The sense of freedom belongs, not to the ego personality that we tend to fixate upon, but from the deeper soul sense that is part of the Spirit here in the manifestation. Sri Aurobindo describes this as follows: "... this freedom and power are influences from the soul. To use a familiar metaphysical language, they type the assent and will of the Purusha without which the Prakriti cannot move on her way. The first and greater part of this soul-influence is in the form of an assent to Nature, an acquiescence; and for good reason. For I start with the action of the universal Energy which the Spirit has set in motion and as I rise from the ignorance towards knowledge, the first thing demanded from me is to gather experience of its law and of my relations to the law and partly therefore to acquiesce, to allow myself to be moved, to see and to come to know the nature of the motions, to suffer and obey the law, to understand and know Karma."

The famous image from the Upanishads comes to mind, wherein there are two birds sitting on a common tree. One of them eats the sweet fruit, while the other watches and provides assent. The bird which eats of the fruit is the Prakriti, the nature, consisting of body, life and mind bound together through the device of the surface personality, the ego, and this bird is bound by the law of Karma, cause and effect, through participating in eating the fruits of past actions. The bird which watches and assents is the Purusha, the deeper true personality which is free of the actions of Karma and is not bound by the fruits of the past.

Sri Aurobindo, *Rebirth and Karma*, Section I, Chapter 9, Karma and Freedom, pp. 84-85

The Soul's Assent and Mastery Over Nature and Karma

As long as we remain rooted in the surface consciousness, including body, life and mind, we are essentially the puppets of Nature and under subjection to the law of Karma. In order to achieve liberation from the bondage of Karma, it is essential that we find and establish our standpoint in the witness consciousness. Sri Aurobindo describes the separation of Purusha and Prakriti. This becomes more and more possible as we achieve higher expressions of consciousness in the evolution from Matter, to Life and then to Mind. "But thinking man who experiences increasingly from generation to generation and from life to life the nature of things and develops reflective knowledge and the sense of his soul in Nature, delivers in her a power of initiating will. He is not bound to her set actualities; he can refuse assent, and the thing in Nature to which it is refused goes on indeed for a time and produces its results by impetus of Karma, but as it runs, it loses power and falls into impotence and desuetude. He can do more, he can command a new action and orientation of his nature. The assent was a manifestation of the power of the soul as giver of the sanction, *anumanta,* but this is a power of the soul as active lord of the nature, *isvara.*

There is an interim period while the soul establishes its poise as master of the Nature that the old actions continue or try to reassert themselves, but eventually they must give way to the new direction and impetus provided by the soul. "The mental being in us can be a learner in the school of freedom, not a perfect adept. A real freedom comes when we get away from the mind into the life of the spirit, from personality o the Person, from Nature to the lord of Nature."

"But if man would have too a freedom of power, of participation, of companionship as the son of God in a greater divine control, he must then not only get back from mind, but must stand, in his thought and will even, above the levels of mentality and find there a station of leverage… whence he can sovereignly move the world of his being. Such a station of consciousness there is in the supramental ranges. When the soul is one with the Supreme and with the universal not only in essence of consciousness and spiritual truth of being, but in expressive act too of consciousness and being, when it enjoys an initiating and relating truth of spiritual will and knowledge and the soul's overflowing delight in God and existence, when it is admitted to the spirit's fullness of asset to self and its creative liberty, its strain of an eternal joy in self-existence ad self-manifestation, Karma itself becomes a rhythm of freedom and birth a strain of immortality."

Sri Aurobindo, *Rebirth and Karma*, Section I, Chapter 9, Karma and Freedom, pp. 85-86

CHAPTER TEN

KARMA, WILL AND CONSEQUENCE

The Will of the Spirit Provides Significance to Existence

As we have determined in our review thus far, the material world is not the origin of existence, but the result of the Spirit's involution of consciousness. It is not a mechanical world absent any deeper significance, but rather, all Matter is instinct with consciousness–there is a precise, highly-organized and intelligent order to Matter and Life. The systematic development of Life out of Matter and Mind out of Life is an unfolding of the Consciousness contained secretly therein. It is with this understanding that we begin to look at the relationship of Will, Karma and consequence in this new chapter.

Sri Aurobindo introduces the subject with a defining statement: "Will, Karma and consequence are the three steps of the Energy which moves the universe. But Karma and consequence are only the outcome of will or even its forms; will gives them their value and without it they would be nothing, nothing at least to man the thinking and growing soul and nothing, it may be hazarded, to the Spirit of which he is a flame and power as well as a creature."

Sri Aurobindo points out that the meaning of this entire existence comes from the will of the Spirit: "But by itself and without the light of an inhabiting will this working is only a huge soulless mechanism, a loud rattling of crank and pulley, a monstrous pounding of spring and piston. It is the presence of the spirit and its will that gives a meaning to the action and it is the value of the result to the soul that gives its profound importance to all great or little consequence."

"Spirit and consciousness and power of the spirit and Ananda are the meaning of existence. Take away this spiritual significance and this world of energy becomes a mechanical fortuity or a blind and rigid Maya."

Sri Aurobindo, *Rebirth and Karma*, Section I, Chapter 10, Karma, Will and Consequence, pg. 87

The Value and Significance of the Role of Man In the Universe

Our view of the role and importance of man in the grand scheme of things has gone through the entire gamut from the one extreme that holds that human beings are simply specks of dust in a vast mechanical machinery, essentially having little or no ultimate value, to the other extreme that places man at the center of creation as the most important of all beings (and many positions between these two extremes). While we may not be able to say, as some have said that "man is the measure of all things", we can nevertheless appreciate that there is a real and significant role for a being that provides conscious awareness, self-reflection and an intuition and aspiration for further evolutionary development.

Sri Aurobindo describes this role in the following way: "The will of man is the agent of the Eternal for the unveiling of his secret meaning in the material creation. Man's mind takes up all the knots of the problem and works them out by the power of the spirit within him and brings them nearer to the full force and degree of their individual and cosmic solutions. This is his dignity and his greatness and he needs no other to justify and give a perfect value to his birth and his acts and his passing and his return to birth, a return which must be–and what is there in it to grieve at or shun?–until the work of the Eternal in him is perfected or the cycles rest from the glory of their labour."

Man's will represents an action of the Eternal in the evolutionary schema and is part of the engine that drives forward the unfolding and expression of ever higher levels of consciousness in the material universe.

Sri Aurobindo, *Rebirth and Karma*, Section I, Chapter 10, Karma, Will and Consequence, pp. 87-88

The Eternal Soul Of Man Acts To
Carry Out the Eternal Will In Manifestation

Sri Aurobindo clarifies the balanced view that neither over-states nor understates the importance and role of man in the universal manifestation: "Man is a conscious soul of the Eternal, one with the Infinite in his inmost being, and the spirit within him is master of his acts and his fate."

When we consider the question of Fate or Karma or any other idea that implies some externally determined result that is either pre-destined or at least guided to a specific result and conclusion, we should consider it from this standpoint. We are not separated from the Eternal and Infinite. We are not therefore simply victims of fate or controlled by Karma.

Sri Aurobindo in fact redefines the concept of fate: "For fate is *fatum*, the form of act and creation declared beforehand by a Will within him and the universe as the thing to be done, to be achieved, to be worked out and made the self-expression of his spiritual being. Fate is *adrsta,* the unseen thing which the Spirit holds hidden in the plan of its vision, the consequence concealed from the travailing mind absorbed in the work of the moment by the curtained nearnesses or the far invisible reaches of Time. Fate is *niyati*, the thing willed and executed by Nature, who is power of the Spirit, according to a fixed law of it self-governed workings."

This obviously changes our view of our role in the universe: "But since this Eternal and Infinite, our greater Self, is also the universal being, man in the universe is inseparably one with all the rest of existence, not a soul working out its isolated spiritual destiny and nature while all other beings are nothing but his environment and means or obstacles,–that they are indeed, but they are much more to him,–which is the impression cast on the mind by the thought or the religions that emphasise too much his centre of individuality or his aim of personal salvation. He is not indeed solely a portion of the universe. He is an eternal soul which, though limited for certain temporal purposes in its outward consciousness, has to learn to enlarge itself out of those limits, to find and make effective its unity with the eternal Spirit who informs and transcends the universe."

Sri Aurobindo, *Rebirth and Karma*, Section I, Chapter 10, Karma, Will and Consequence, pg. 88

The Surface Personality and the Inner Person: Bound Will and Free Will

If we consider carefully the wellsprings of action in our surface personality, we find that there is no reality to the concept of free will, and that our actions are conditioned and determined by both our individual karmic chain of past consequences, and by the impact of the universal being of which we are a part on our action. We like to believe that we are somehow separate and distinct from this universal manifestation, and that we can thereby be free of its influence, but this is an illusion, not a reality. Sri Aurobindo discusses this issue: "The dealings of our will with Karma and consequence have to be envisaged in the light of this double truth of man's individuality and man's universality." and "It becomes clear enough that our ego, our outward personality can be only a minor, a temporal, an instrumental form of our being. The will of the ego, the outward, the mentally personal will which acts in the movement cannot be free in any complete or separate sense of freedom. It cannot so be free because it is bound by its partial and limited nature and it is shaped by the mechanism of its ignorance, and again because it is an individualised form and working of the universal energy and at every moment impinged upon and modified and largely shaped by environing wills and powers and forces."

The inner person, connected to the transcendent and the universal Being that is manifesting and unfolding the universal creation, partakes of the freedom of the Spirit and is one with the consciousness that directs and drives the manifestation.

"The inward will in the being which is in intimacy with that Power is the real will and this outward thing only an instrumentation for a working out from moment to moment, a spring of the karmic mechanism. That inward will we find when we get back to it, to be a free will, not armoured in a separate liberty, but free in harmony with the freedom of the Spirit guiding and compelling Nature in all souls and in all happenings."

Sri Aurobindo, *Rebirth and Karma*, Section I, Chapter 10, Karma, Will and Consequence, pp. 88-90

The Acts of the Moment
Are Created By the Eternal Soul

There is a proverb about not being able to see the forest for the trees. The focus on the individual details makes us lose sight of the "big picture", the sense or significance, the perspective. Impressionist painters such as Vincent Van Gogh conveyed this sense through their artistic efforts. Up close, their paintings overwhelm one with the incredible number of brush strokes, texture, and color. There is however a "tipping point" as one backs away from the canvas where one suddenly switches from the "detail view" to the "gestalt", the idea being conveyed, and suddenly the "big picture" takes over and the brush strokes are seen for what they are, the technique or the "facts" by which a larger significance is expressed.

Similarly, we become so involved in and overwhelmed by the detailed acts of our day to day lives that we tend not to recognize the "big picture", the significance of those lives or those acts.

Sri Aurobindo discusses this situation with a very insightful view about the relationship between the day to day details and the soul's meaning in creating and carrying out those details: "To understand one must cease to dwell exclusively on the act and will of the moment and its immediate consequences. Our present will and personality are bound by many things, by our physical and vital heredity, by a past creation of our mental nature, environmental forces, by limitation, by ignorance. But our soul behind is greater and older than our present personality. The soul is not the result of our heredity, but has prepared by its own action and affinities this heredity. It has drawn around it these environmental forces by past karma and consequence. It has created in other lives the mental nature of which now it makes use."

Just as we undergo a transformation in our view of life when we understand that the sun does not revolve around the earth, but the earth around the sun; and that the entire solar system is part of an enormous Milky Way Galaxy which is a part of a larger universe, we can begin to understand the soul's action and the true meaning of the details of our day to day lives when we take a different standpoint outside the focus on each of the details and begin to view the "big picture". Modern psychologists point out that there are essentially two hemispheres to the human brain. Left brain activity tends to be fixated on details, analysis and "the trees" of our lives; while right brain activity looks at the "gestalt", the "big picture", "the forest" if you will. Both of these perspectives are valuable, but they must be integrated in order to give a true sense and meaning to what we experience.

Sri Aurobindo points out "To live in this knowledge is not to take away the value and potency of the moment's will and act, but to give it an immensely increased meaning and importance....Our every thought, will, action carries with it its power of future self-determination and is too a help or a hindrance for the spiritual evolution of those around us and a force in the universal working. For the soul in us takes in the influences it receives from others for its own self-determination and gives out influences which the soul in them uses for their growth and experience. Our individual life becomes an immensely greater thing in itself and is convinced too of an abiding unity with the march of the universe."

Sri Aurobindo, *Rebirth and Karma*, Section I, Chapter 10, Karma, Will and Consequence, pg. 90

The Broader Implications
Of Karma and Consequence

When we look at Karma through the lens of perspective, we can see that our usual interpretation of Karma and its effects, focused solely on its impact on our own lives or the most part, is just as faulty as our too narrow view of the role of the individual. Karma and consequence are not solely individual. Just as we are connected to both the universal manifestation through oneness, and our soul is part and parcel of the Eternal manifesting here, so Karma also takes on the aspect of acting on the individual and universal levels. We can find the meaning of karmic consequence not solely in its impact on our limited personality and limited life, but on the lives of others and the entire universal existence.

Sri Aurobindo describes the interaction thus: "At present we fix too much on the particular will and act of the moment and a particular consequence in a given time. But the particular only receives its value by all of which it is a part, all from which it comes, all to which it moves. We fix too much also on the externalities of karma and consequence, this good or that bad action and result of action. But the real consequence which the soul is after is a growth in the manifestation of its being, an enlarging of its range and action of power, its comprehension of delight of being, its delight of creation and self-creation, and not only its own but the same things in others with which its greater becoming and joy are one. Karma and consequence draw their meaning from their value to the soul; they are steps by which it moves towards the perfection of its manifested nature. And even when this object is won, our action need not cease, for it will keep its value and be a greater force of help for all these others with whom in self we are one."

This opens the door to individual implications to the function of karma in the manifestation as well as universal impacts, and an ever-progressing development, both for the individual and the world within which he acts.

Sri Aurobindo, *Rebirth and Karma*, Section I, Chapter 10, Karma, Will and Consequence, pp. 90-91

The Immeasurable Delight of the Liberated Being and Its Liberated Action

If there is one frequently recurring theme throughout human history with respect to our effort and its significance, it is that whatever we do on earth is a struggle, a form of suffering, a travail, and eventually we need to abandon this life and work to identify ourselves with the eternal and end the suffering. This theme we find in the illusionist philosophies of Mayavada, as well as in the Buddhist direction, and also in the Christian focus on other-worldly salvation or even the redemption and bliss found in the Muslim heaven. Whatever temporary role or significance our human life has is overshadowed by the eventual need to go beyond.

Sri Aurobindo, however, comes to a completely different conclusion. Since he recognizes the action of life as the expression of the unfolding of the creative energy and consciousness of the eternal Spirit, he does not find any need to deny a significance to the individual or the collective life, or to see it as an expression of the Spirit's enjoyment of existence.

"The spirit we are is not only an eternal consciousness and eternal being; its characters are an eternal power of being and an eternal Ananda. Creation is not to the spirit a trouble and an anguish, but a delight expressed, even though in the entirety of its depths inexpressible, fathomless, endless, inexhaustible. It is only the limited action of mind in the ignorance straining after possession and discovery and unable to find the concealed power of the spirit that makes of the delight of action and creation a passion or suffering: for, limited in capacity and embarrassed by life and body, it has yet desires beyond its capacity, because it is the instrument of a growth and the seed of an illimitable self-expression and it has the pain of the growth and the pain of the insufficiency of its action and delight. But let this struggling self-creator and doer of works once grow into the consciousness and power of the secret infinite spirit within it and all this passion and suffering passes away into an immeasurable delight of liberated being and its liberated action."

Sri Aurobindo, *Rebirth and Karma*, Section I, Chapter 10, Karma, Will and Consequence, pg. 91

Decoupling Karma From Suffering

Much of our view of the nature of Karma, and its inevitable link to the experience of suffering is due to the Buddhist explanation of this connection. The experience of the Buddha was a key step forward in our ability to begin to separate ourselves from the surface personality and begin to seek and, eventually, find a standpoint outside the limited human experience. The impetus for this seeking was the formula that all action creates karma, and that all karma ties us to the experience of suffering.

Sri Aurobindo points out that it is not sufficient to stop with this experience, as it does not encompass the entire realm of possibilities, the true freedom beyond the limits of human surface nature, wherein one finds not only peace and separation, but the true power and consciousness of the eternal Existence that founds and creates all existence.

"To find self is the cure of suffering, because self is infinite possession and perfect satisfaction. But to find self in quiescence is not the whole meaning of the spiritual evolution, but to find it too in its power of being; for being is not only eternal status, but also eternal movement, not only rest, but also action. There is a delight of rest and a delight of action, but in the wholeness of the spirit these two things are no longer contraries, but one and inseparable. The status of the spirit is an eternal calm, but also it self-expression in world-being is without any beginning or end, because eternal power means an eternal creation. When we gain the one, we need not lose its counterpart and consequence. To get to a foundation is not to destroy all capacity for superstructure."

"Karma is nothing but the will of the Spirit in action, consequence nothing more but the creation of will."

"When the will is limited in mind, karma appears as a bondage and a limitation, consequence as a reaction or an imposition. But when the will of te being is infinite in the spirit, karma and consequence become instead the joy of the creative spirit, the construction of the eternal mechanist, the word and drama of the eternal poet, the harmony of the eternal musician, the play of the eternal child. This lesser, bound, seemingly separate evolution is only a step in the free self-creation of the Spirit from its own illimitable Ananda. That is behind all we are and do; to hide it from mind and bring it slowly forward into the front of existence and action is the present play of Self with Nature."

Sri Aurobindo, *Rebirth and Karma*, Section I, Chapter 10, Karma, Will and Consequence, pp. 91-92

CHAPTER ELEVEN

REBIRTH AND KARMA

The Concepts of Rebirth and Karma Require One Another For Meaning

Once we recognize a law of Karma, a sequence of cause and effect, we come reasonably quickly to the conclusion that it can only have a real meaning within the context of multiple births. Similarly if we start from the concept of rebirth, we find that there must be some linking between the births that provides significance as well, and this linking is the "law of Karma". Either way, we find that the one concept requires the other.

We see around us an ordered universe, with subtlety and inter-related and inter-operable parts that clearly are part of some larger whole, both in terms of the universal manifestation and in terms of the sequence of actions over time. Such an organization speaks to a creative Intelligence and a pattern to the manifestation which implies meaning and significance, not a chaotic wild dream sequence or some kind of illusory existence.

Sri Aurobindo discusses the link between the concepts in this next chapter, Rebirth and Karma: "These two things are the soul side and the nature side of one and the same cosmic sequence. Rebirth is meaningless without karma, and karma has no fount of inevitable origin and no rational and no moral justification if i is not an instrumentality for the sequences of the soul's continuous experience. If we believe that the soul is repeatedly reborn in the body, we must believe also that there is some link between the lives that preceded and the lives that follow and that the past of the soul has an effect on its future; and that is the spiritual essence of the law of Karma."

"The continuous existence of the soul in rebirth must signify an evolution if not of the self, for that is said to be immutable, yet of its more outward active soul or self of experience. This evolution is not possible if there is not a connected sequence

from life to life, a result of action and experience, an evolutionary consequence to the soul, a law of Karma."

Sri Aurobindo, *Rebirth and Karma*, Section I, Chapter 11, Rebirth and Karma, pg. 93

The Law of Karma Is More
Than a Mechanical Law of Cause and Effect

Karma is frequently understood to be a law of cause and effect, but rarely do we dig deeper to understand how this works. This leads to a lot of generalizations that may not be entirely correct when examined more closely. One of these generalizations tends to treat the action of Karma as some kind of automatic cause/effect mechanism such as we see in the laws of physics expounded by the early Western physicists. "For every action there is an equal and opposite reaction" for instance, as well as the mechanical laws of motion, mass and momentum. If it were only that simple!

While we are treating Karma as some kind of mechanism, we also want it to have a moral and ethical component, but we now have something of a conflict. In the physical world, a "cause" may lead to an effect that redounds, not upon the "doer" but on some other party who perhaps was innocent and unaware of the action. For instance, a mountain climber could make a loud sound in a glacier region and trigger an avalanche which buried a number of people, but not the person who instigated it! We can come up with any number of scenarios where "cause and effect" on the physical plane clearly visits its results on others than those undertaking the initiating action.

To understand the complexity of what is intended by the concept of Karma, and its necessary connection to the process of rebirth, we need to step back from the purely mechanical aspects and see it as an implementation mechanism for the evolutionary development that takes place through rebirth to bring about the development of consciousness in a systematic outflowering through Time.

"Karma is action, there is a thing done and a doer and an active consequence; these three are the three joints, the three locks, the three *sandhis* of the connexus of Karma. And it is a complex mental, moral and physical working; for the law of it is not less true of the mental and moral than of the physical consequence of the act to the doer. The will and the idea are the driving force of the action, and the momentum does not come from some commotion in my chemical atoms or some working of ion and electron or some weird biological effervescence. Therefore the act and consequence must have some relation to the will and the idea and there must be a mental and moral consequence to the soul which has the will and idea. That, if we admit the individual as a real being, signifies a continuity of act and consequence to him and therefore rebirth for a field of this working. It is evident that in one life we do not and cannot labour out and exhaust all the values and powers of that life, but only carry on a past thread, weave out something in the present, prepare infinitely more for the future."

Sri Aurobindo, *Rebirth and Karma*, Section I, Chapter 11, Rebirth and Karma, pp. 93-94

Individual Karma, Collective Karma and Universal Karma

For those who hold that there is only an "All-Soul" and no reality to the individual soul, there is clearly no rationale for there being any necessity for rebirth, as the growth, and reaping of consequences at the individual level basically would have no meaning. There would be an "All-Soul" undertaking actions through innumerable forms and beings, and it would not really matter that the consequences would fall on others, or on future generations, rather than the individual carrying out the action.

We actually can see that the action of the individual can and does impact not just the individual undertaking the action, but others, both in the present and in the future. Some religious or philosophical directions have created colorful descriptions around this phenomenon when they speak of the "sins of the father being visited on the sons" down through many generations.

The impact on the individual becomes real, and requires rebirth for its effectuation, if we attribute a reality to the individual soul. The impact on others nevertheless still occurs and becomes what we may describe as something of a "collective Karma". Sri Aurobindo discusses this with the following: "What I sow in this hour, is reaped by my posterity for several generations and we can then call it the karma of the family. What the men of today as community or people resolve upon and execute, comes back with a blessing or a sword upon the future of their race when they themselves have passed away and are no longer there to rejoice or to suffer; and that we can speak of as the karma of the nation. Mankind as a whole too has a karma; what it wrought in its past, will shape its future destiny; individuals seem only to be temporary units of human thought, will, nature who act according to the compulsion of the soul in humanity and disappear; but the karma of the race which thy have helped to form continues through the centuries, the millenniums, the cycles."

Of course, this form of collective karma is not the entire picture, and the life and karma of the individual is inter-woven with the life of the society, with impacts moving in both directions and reflecting the evolutionary development through the operation of Time.

Sri Aurobindo, *Rebirth and Karma*, Section I, Chapter 11, Rebirth and Karma, pp. 94-95

The Individual and the Universal Are Aspects of One Eternal Being

Due to the habitual action of mind to divide and fragment, we tend to look at things as "either/or" options and to then set up clear demarcations between one thing and another. This action has been extremely useful when it comes to analyzing and breaking down a complex set of processes into distinct steps and thereby gain the ability to act in the material world. However, it has a tendency to overlook the factors that unify and integrate into a larger whole, a "gestalt", the "big picture", and it is just this integrated viewpoint which Sri Aurobindo takes pains to enunciate while at the same time not undervaluing the analytical mind's contribution.

"For the original and eternal Reality, the Alpha and Omega, the Godhead is neither separate in the individual nor is he only and solely a Pantheos, a cosmic spirit. He is at once the eternal individual and the eternal All-Soul of this and many universes, and at the same time he is much more than these things."

"The universe finds itself in me, even as I find myself in the universe, because we are this face and that face of the one eternal Reality, and individual being is as much needed as universal being to work out this manifestation. The individual vision of things is as true as the universal vision, both are ways of the self-seeing of the Eternal."

There is no actual conflict here with modern science, inasmuch as science focuses on working out the details of the manifestation and does not thereby contradict the "big picture" view. In fact, the further modern science explores the material universe, the closer it comes to an understanding of the spiritual Truth of existence. Starting from the viewpoint of "all this is Matter", scientists subsequently advanced to the view that "Matter is Energy." From there the next leap was that "Energy is Consciousness". Today scientists are beginning to explore the question of Consciousness and advancing concepts of universal creation that bring us to the frontiers of spirituality with a unified field and complex manifestation of multiple universes contained within one all-embracing consciousness.

Sri Aurobindo, *Rebirth and Karma*, Section I, Chapter 11, Rebirth and Karma, pp. 95-96

The Principle of Uniqueness
In the Manifestation

Sri Aurobindo has identified a persistent principle of the manifestation that becomes ever more apparent as we ascend the scale of consciousness, and that is the principle of "uniqueness" which is intimately bound up with the necessity of rebirth. It is in the end, the uniqueness of the individual that presents the hidden thread of development that cannot be accomplished through one lifetime. We see the start of the differentiation process as the unity of the life force begins to develop into different species of plant and animal life, what we might consider to be the development of a group consciousness that manifests characteristics that are unique compared to other species. Eventually, however, we see the further development, particularly as the principle of Mind takes hold, of unique individuals within the group who begin to develop and express characteristics that make that individual different from the rest of the common group.

"...this uniqueness is everywhere, but appears as a subordinate factor only in the lower ranges of existence. It becomes more and more important and pronounced as we rise in the scale, enlarges in mind, gets to enormous proportions when we come to the things of the spirit. That would seem to indicate that the cause of this significant uniqueness is something bound up with the very nature of spirit; it is something it held in itself and is bringing out more and more as it emerges out of material Nature into self-conscience."

The first sign, the development of the group or collective variation, also leads to the concept of a group or collective karma. "For the group or collective soul renews and prolongs itself and in man at least develops its nature and experience from generation to generation." Wherever there is persistence of a particular type of manifestation, there is a cause-effect development that carries out the law we have called "karma".

"...the action and development of the whole produces consequences of karma and experience for the individual and the totality even as the action and development of the individual produces consequences and experience for others, for the group, for the whole."

"The communal soul-variation mounts up from the rest, exceeds, brings in or brings out something more, something new, adds novel powers in the evolution. The individual mounts and exceeds in the same way from the community. It is in him, on his highest heights that we get the flame-crest of self-manifestation by which the One finds himself in Nature."

Sri Aurobindo, *Rebirth and Karma*, Section I, Chapter 11, Rebirth and Karma, pp. 96-97

The Interaction of the Individual Soul, Heredity and Environment

We are born into the world as children of our parents, carrying with us a physical heritage from our ancestors which is called heredity. These traits are passed along in the DNA transmitted from the parents, and combined according to the dominant or recessive characteristics of the particular genetic interactions. This process therefore provides a basis for the continuity of the physical framework of our lives from generation to generation. The ability for genetic material to combine and create new combinations through the contribution of the two parents provides an enormous potential capability for individuation and new development in the newly born child.

This process of heredity, however, is not the sole factor in determining our lives. Once born into the world, we interact with an environment consisting of both the world at large, and the other beings with whom we interact. We are both influenced, and in our turn, influence the development of the community of life and existence and its development. We are part of the community and partake of the time-spirit within which we are born and live, carried along by the currents of that tremendous collective energy, but also doing our part to try to shape and move that collective existence.

While there is a debate about whether heredity or environment is more important in the development of the human being, and there are strong proponents of each view, it is clear that both are part of the legacy of the past, and the force of the present within which we have to take up our lives and become who we are meant to be. These two factors on their own however are not the whole story, although they provide us a clue. When we recognize that the very process helps to ensure "uniqueness" of each individual, we can see that the physical process supports the concept of the individual soul born into life.

Sri Aurobindo concludes the following with respect to heredity: "What matters supremely is what I make of my heredity and not what my heredity makes of me." With respect to environment: "What is supremely important is what I make of all this surrounding and invading present and not what it makes of me." The individual importance is recognized: "Still the central power of my psychology takes its colour from this seeing that I

live for my self, and for others or for the world only as an extension of my self, as a thing with which I am bound up in some
kind of oneness. I seem to be a soul, self or spirit who constantly
with the assistance of all create out of my past and present my
future being and myself too help in the surrounding creative
evolution."

Sri Aurobindo, *Rebirth and Karma*, Section I, Chapter 11, Rebirth and Karma, pp. 97-98

The Interaction of Soul, Rebirth and Karma

When we observe the workings of Nature, we see processes that are worked out in intricate detail and which can span aeons of time in their working. Even short-lived creatures are part of a much larger fabric of life which itself spans long periods of time and which encompasses what came before and sets the stage for what comes after. We see no evidence of any caprice or happenstance in this organized rolling-out of the manifestation. It is therefore unlikely and highly suspect to assume that the Soul which we either intuit or actually experience as providing an independent actor in this development is something that suddenly appears without any precedent, or disappears without any trace after one lifetime.

Sri Aurobindo takes up this issue: "It is reasonable to suppose that this powerful independent element which supervenes and works upon the physical and vital evolution, was in the past and will be in the future. It is reasonable also to suppose that it did not come in suddenly from some unconnected existence and does not pass out after one brief intervention; its close connection with the life of the world is rather a continuation of a long past connection. And this brings in at once the whole necessity of past birth and karma. I am a persistent being who pursue my evolution within the persistent being of the world. I have evolved my human birth and I help constantly in the human evolution. I have created by my past karma my own conditions and my relations with the life of others and the general karma. That shapes my heredity, my environment, my affinities, my connections, my material, my opportunities and obstacles, a part of my predestined powers and results, not arbitrarily predestined but predetermined by my own stage of nature and past action, and on this groundwork I build new karma and farther strengthen or subtilise my power of natural being, woven in with the universal evolution and all its lines are included in the web of being, but it is not merely a jutting point or moment of it or a brief tag shot into the tissue."

We see here a coherent and organized process that provides a clear sense of the soul's evolutionary effort through the mechanism of karma, cause and effect, carried out through time by the operation of the systematic rebirth of the soul.

Sri Aurobindo, *Rebirth and Karma*, Section I, Chapter 11, Rebirth and Karma, pp. 98-99

The Individual and the Universal

Sri Aurobindo's view of rebirth takes issue with the near-exclusive concentration laid upon the concept in the traditional viewpoint. This traditional viewpoint looks upon life on the earth as some kind of short-term interlude, with the goal being to return to the original source and therein to dissolve ourselves. The entire focus then revolves around individual salvation. It is, however, impossible to understand the larger significance of the manifestation and evolution of the world and all the other beings in the world from a viewpoint that starts with this level of fragmentation. This has led many to consider the world to be an illusion. Sri Aurobindo integrates the evolutionary development of the individual with the universal manifestation.

"Certain it is that while we are here, our rebirth or karma, even while it runs on its own lines, is intimately one with the same lines in the universal existence. But my self-knowledge and self-finding too do not abolish my oneness with other life and other beings. An intimate universality is part of the glory of spiritual perfection. This idea of universality, of oneness not only with God or the eternal Self in me, but with all humanity and other beings, is growing to be the most prominent strain in our minds and it has to be taken more largely into account in any future idea or computation of the significance of rebirth and karma. It was admitted in old time; the Buddhist law of compassion was a recognition of its importance; but it has to be given a still more pervading power in the general significance."

Sri Aurobindo, *Rebirth and Karma*, Section I, Chapter 11, Rebirth and Karma, pp. 99-100

Rebirth and Karma Work Out the Spirit's Self-Effectuation In the World

Sri Aurobindo has provided us a succinct summary of the meaning and functioning of rebirth and karma within the manifestation.

"The self-effectuation of the Spirit in the world is the truth on which we take our foundation, a great, a long self-weaving in time. Rebirth is the continuity of that self-effectuation in the individual, the persistence of the thread; Karma is the process, a force, a work of energy and consequence in the material world, an inner and an outer will, an action and mental, moral, dynamic consequence in the soul evolution of which the material world is a constant scene."

With this principle stated, the rest remains a matter of the detailed methodology of this self-effectuation and the actual working out of the various details of the law of karma and the process of rebirth. We can expect that the details will act to carry out the larger meaning and intention of the manifestation of the Spirit.

Sri Aurobindo, *Rebirth and Karma*, Section I, Chapter 11, Rebirth and Karma, pg. 100

Chapter Twelve

Karma and Justice

Introduction To the Lines of Karma

Perhaps the most intriguing questions for most of us are those that relate to the operation of the law of Karma. We want Karma to conform to our mental notions of right and wrong, or to fit within a pattern that satisfies our desires. We expect to find some kind of "legal system" that operates the law of Karma and to find thereby that our moral, ethical, religious or mental notions are supported and justified by the action of Karma.

The law of Karma however is not a law framed by the mind of man, but a law of the Spirit that has manifested the complexity and subtlety of the entire creation. Sri Aurobindo describes the framework of Karma: "The law of Karma can be no rigid and mechanical canon or rough practical rule of thumb, but rather its guiding principle should be as supple a harmonist as the Spirit itself whose will of self-knowledge it embodies and should adapt itself to the need of self-development of the variable individual souls who are feeling their way along its lines towards the right balance, synthesis, harmonics of their action. The karmic idea cannot be–for spirit and not mind is its cause–a cosmic reflection of our limited average human intelligence, but rather the law of a greater spiritual wisdom, a means which behind all its dumb occult appearances embodies an understanding lead and a subtle management towards our total perfection."

We should therefore examine the law of Karma with a wide understanding and an open mind in order to discover its true significance and not simply overlay our mental notions on this spiritual principle.

Sri Aurobindo, *Rebirth and Karma*, Section I, Chapter 12, Karma and Justice, pg. 101

A Karmic Banking System?

The law of Karma is most often thought of as some kind of ethical legal or banking system meting out exact rewards for our good and bad acts. The determination of virtue and vice for this system is of course based on our own cultural biases and limitations of vision, and the framework is one which tries to justify what happens to us in our lives. If the bad seem to prosper or the good to suffer, we need to find a satisfactory explanation and the law of Karma is therefore viewed through the prism of our limited viewpoint in our limited lives. At the same time, we do "good" because we expect a reward and avoid "bad" because we fear punishment.

Sri Aurobindo describes this common idea about the law of Karma: "Its idea of karma is a mechanical and materialistic ethics, a crudely exact legal judgment and administration of reward and punishment, an external sanction to virtue and prohibition of sin, a code, a balance. The idea is that there must be a justice governing the award of happiness and misery on the earth, a humanly intelligible equity and that the law of Karma represents it and gives us its formula. I have done so much good, *punya* . It is my capital, my accumulation and balance. I must have it paid out to me in so much coin of prosperity, the legal currency of this sovereign and divine Themis, or why on earth should I at all do good? I have done so much evil. That too must come back to me in so much exact and accurate punishment and misfortune. There must be so much outward suffering or an inward suffering caused by outward event and pressure; for if there were not this physically sensible, visible, inevitable result, where would be any avenging justice and where could we find any deterrent sanction in Nature against evil? And this award is that of an exact judge, a precise administrator, a scrupulous merchant of good for good and evil for evil who has learned nothing and will never learn anything of the Christian or Buddhistic ideal rule, has no bowels of mercy or compassion, no forgiveness for sin, but holds austerely to an eternal Mosaic law, eye for eye, tooth for tooth, a full, slow or swift, but always calm and precisely merciless *lex talionis*.

Sri Aurobindo, *Rebirth and Karma*, Section I, Chapter 12, Karma and Justice, pp. 101-102

The Story of the Karmic Accountant

Sri Aurobindo illustrates the absurdity of some of the most popular conceptions about the operation of the law of Karma with a story from the press of his day.

It was a story of a "rich man who had violently deprived another of his substance. The victim is born as the son of the oppressor and in the delirium of a fatal illness reveals that he has obliged his old tyrant and present father to spend on him and so lose the monetary equivalent of the property robbed minus a certain sum, but that sum must be paid now, otherwise–The debt is absolved and as the last pice is expended, the reborn soul departs, for its sole object in taking birth is satisfied, accounts squared and the spirit of Karma content."

Sri Aurobindo explains that this view develops the mechanical system to its logical conclusion and to an extreme, to the point that apparently "the precise accountant becomes very like an unconscionable hundred per cent usurer." This is based on the fact that in this story the rewards for virtue take place both in heaven after death, and on earth after rebirth, while the punishment for sin also occurs both beyond and in the next birth, thus indicating a double punishment or a double reward.

Clearly the system illustrated by this story does not stand close scrutiny and cannot provide us any basis in reality for our understanding of the law of Karma.

Sri Aurobindo, *Rebirth and Karma*, Section I, Chapter 12, Karma and Justice, pg. 102

Ethics, Desire and Karma

It is quite natural for the vital nature of man to desire success, well-being, vital fulfilment in our lives. This involves the achievement of pleasure and the avoidance of suffering. This actually acts as the motive spring or impulsion behind our actions in the vast majority of cases. We have framed our ethical concepts to incorporate the satisfaction of these impulsions, and thus have created a measure for our ethical framework that insists on such achievement.

Sri Aurobindo points out, however, that ethics as a conceptual principle can be seen, and should be recognized, in the absence of specific attainment of desire. In fact, an ethical framework tied to overt or subtle achievement of pleasure or avoidance of suffering is more in the nature of a bargain than a truly ethical act. "...true ethics is dharma, the right fulfilment and working of the higher nature, and right action should have right motive, should be its own justification and not go limping on the crutches of greed and fear. Right done for its own sake is truly ethical and ennobles the growing spirit; right done in the lust for a material reward or from fear of the avenging stripes of the executioner or sentence of the judge, may be eminently practical and useful for the moment, but it is not in the least degree ethical, but is rather a lowering of the soul of man; or at least the principle is a concession to his baser animal and unspiritual nature."

Human law is tailored to more or less conform to the expectation of desire and mete out punishment for acts which cause pain and suffering, and reward those who act within the framework or who have been victimized by acts deemed worthy of punishment.

The law of Karma, as popularly conceived, "...is expected...to deal with man on his own principle and do this very thing with a much sterner and more inescapable firmness of application and automatic necessity of consequence." Thus, we have created the cosmic law in the image of our human law, and turned it, in our normal view of the matter, into a system of meted out rewards and punishments.

Sri Aurobindo, *Rebirth and Karma*, Section I, Chapter 12, Karma and Justice, pp. 102-103

Ethics, Karma and Cosmic Law

The popular notion of the law of Karma implies that somehow our human conception of justice in return for our actions is expanded, extended and fulfilled in the cosmic law. We see however that in various cultures, at various points of time, there are different views about "right and wrong" and different implementations of justice. Clearly we cannot simply extrapolate our human notions and overlay them onto the entire cosmic existence.

We may see this tendency as another example of our anthropocentric tendencies; that is, we always try to place ourselves at the center of the universe and judge everything by our limited viewpoint. This tendency used to hold that the earth was at the center of the universe, and that the sun revolved around the earth. We now know that such conceptions are inaccurate and a reflection of the limitations of human perception and understanding, rather than a true representation of the working of the solar system. Similarly, our notions of ethics, justice, and Karma suffer from a similar limitation and it is time for us to shift our viewpoint and expand our understanding so as not to be caught in the fallacy of trying to create God in man's image in yet another field of review.

When we observe the working of cosmic law, we can see that our human conception of reward for ethical or virtuous acts, and punishment for the opposite does not hold up universally as we would want and expect it to, another indication of the limitation of the attempt to overlay human, mental frameworks on the universal existence!

The idealised view of ethics, which sets up a standard of action that is not rooted in the fulfillment of desire, clearly does not lead to any universally observable truth of the cosmic action. Sri Aurobindo describes its role in such a viewpoint thus: "That more elevated action, it would almost seem, is an ideal movement of less use for the practical governance of life than as one part of a preparation for a fourth and last need of man, his need of spiritual salvation, and salvation winds up finally our karma and casts away the economy along with the very thought and will of life."

The paradigm in this view is "Desire is the law of life and action and therefore of Karma. To do things above the material level for their own sake and their pure right or pure delight is to head straight towards the distances of heaven or the silence of the Ineffable." In other words, ethics is not so much a rule for living out our lives as for abandoning the life of the world for a higher and other life of the Spirit. This view has in fact gained substantial adherence throughout the world's religious and spiritual traditions. Sri Aurobindo asks us to consider, however, that there may be further, more complete formulations that do not abandon life, but fulfill it.

Sri Aurobindo, *Rebirth and Karma*, Section I, Chapter 12, Karma and Justice, pp. 103-104

Laws of Nature and Moral Law

While we can recognize that the mental viewpoint that associates our actions with moral or ethical consequences does not appear to be entirely correct, it is nevertheless a fact that there must be some underlying truth to which our viewpoint is connected, however distorted or incomplete our current view may be. Sri Aurobindo undertakes a review of the laws of Nature as we can understand them to help sort out this underlying truth from the accretions of the mental and vital nature which may distort it.

"First, it is sure that Nature has laws of which the observance leads to or helps well-being and of which the violation imposes suffering; but all of them cannot be given a moral significance. Then there is the certainty that there must be a moral law of cause and consequence in the total web of her weaving and this we would perhaps currently put into the formula that good produces good and evil evil, which is a proposition of undoubted truth, though also we see in this complicated world that evil comes out of what we hold to be good, and again out of evil disengages itself something that yet turns to good."

The complications we see here indicate a level of complexity that goes beyond the human mental view, and which also adheres to the larger universal manifestation and thus does not necessarily fit neatly into the framework that we want to fence around the laws of Nature. Further, it must be recognized that human mental considerations of good and evil are somewhat adaptable through time and circumstance. Finally we need to recognize that there may be some level of confusion of different orders of results in our view of the consequences of actions, karma. Each of these elements needs to be disengaged in order to gain a more true perspective of the laws of Nature in operation and to understand the relativity of our attempts to define moral law within our mental framework and then impose it on the universe.

"Perhaps our system of values is too rigidly precise or too narrowly relative; there are subtle things in the totality, minglings, interrelations, cross-currents, suppressed or hidden significances which we do not take into account. The formula is true, but is not the whole truth, at least as now understood in its first superficial significance."

Sri Aurobindo, *Rebirth and Karma*, Section I, Chapter 12, Karma and Justice, pg. 104

Moral Acts Create Primarily Moral Karma

One of the confusions that tends to permeate the discussion about the law of Karma is the implication that because one is morally or ethically good, that one should therefore have physical pleasure or well-being. Sri Aurobindo exposes this confusion and points out that each type of action has its result primarily within its own sphere, and only secondarily will have effects of a different nature.

"...in the ordinary notion of Karma we are combining two different notions of good. I can well understand that moral good does or ought to produce and increase moral good and moral evil to farther and to create moral evil. It does so in myself. The habit of love confirms and enhances my power of love; it purifies my being and opens it to the universal good. The habit of hatred on the contrary corrupts my being, fills it with poison, with bad and morbid toxic matter, and opens it to the general power of evil. My love ought also by a prolongation or a return to produce love in others and my hatred to give rise to hatred; that happens to a certain, a great extent, but it need not be and is not an invariable or rigorous consequence; still we may well see and believe that love does throw out widening ripples and helps to elevate the world while hatred has the opposite consequence. But what is the necessary connection between this good and evil on the one hand and on the other pleasure and pain? Must the ethical power always turn perfectly into some term of kindred hedonistic result? Not entirely; for love is a joy in itself, but also love suffers; hatred is a troubled and self-afflicting thing, but has too its own perverse delight of itself and its gratifications; but in the end we may say that love, because it is born of the universal Delight, triumphs in its own nature and hatred because it is a denial or perversion, leads to a greater sum of misery to myself as to others."

The direct impact of moral or ethical action is thus primarily in the field of moral and ethical result, with tangential and secondary effects in other forms of energy possible, but not necessarily supremely powerful in those other fields. Modern research shows, for instance, that strong emotions, such as love or hatred, release various biochemical reactions, such as stimulating hormones, which can indeed impact the physical body and its ultimate health, positively or negatively as the case may be, but such effects may be offset or overcome by specific direct actions taken to support physical health and well-being or not.

Sri Aurobindo, *Rebirth and Karma*, Section I, Chapter 12, Karma and Justice, pp. 104-105

Karma Is a Complex
Interaction, Not a Mechanical Law

Our surface nature, impelled by the force of desire, wants to believe that the law of karma operates in such a way as to provide material prosperity and well-being in return for our good acts in the realm of moral and ethical conduct; and similarly, that our bad acts ethically or morally will yield to us concrete harm in some outwardly visible way. The law of Karma however appears to be much more subtle and complex than this simplistic view, however appealing to our sense of vital rightness, can explain.

Sri Aurobindo frames the question that arises: "But where is the firm link of correspondence between the ethical and the more vital and physical hedonistic powers of life? How does my ethical good turn into smiling fortune, crowned prosperity, sleek material good and happiness to myself and my ethical evil into frowning misfortune, rugged adversity, sordid material ill and suffering,–for that is what the desire soul of man and the intelligence governed by it seem to demand,–and how is the account squared or the transmutation made between these two very different energies of the affirmation and denial of good?"

We can see that effort made in one field primarily yields results in that field, although it is clear that there are influences from one to another. We may act in a morally positive or negative way and this has an impact in the world around us, in some cases causing joy or suffering in others affected by those acts. In some cases we can even see and recognize a response, more or less according to one of the basic laws of physics, that for each action there is an equal and opposite reaction. But it is difficult to see an exact balancing account, particularly when we are looking for a reaction of a different order or type of energy than that which was put out.

"But this mechanical rebound is not the whole principle of Karma. Nor is Karma wholly a mixed ethical-hedonistic order in its total significance, for there are involved other powers of our consciousness and being. Nor is it again a pure mechanism which we set going by our will and have then helplessly to accept the result; for the will which produced the effect, can also intervene to modify it. And above all the initiating and receiving consciousness can change the values and utilities of the reactions and make another thing of life than this automatic mechanism of fateful return or retribution to the half-blind embodied actor in a mute necessity of rigorous law of Nature."

Sri Aurobindo, *Rebirth and Karma*, Section I, Chapter 12, Karma and Justice, pp. 105-106

Overcoming the Reward and Punishment View of the Law of Karma

We focus generally on the law of Karma in the light of our nature of desire. We seek pleasure and try to avoid pain. We want to be rewarded and we want to avoid punishment. This is the nature of the desire-soul in man that is based on the vital principles of attraction and repulsion, with an underlying principle of desire. We therefore tend to see the law of Karma as an external representation of this desire-soul's focus, and thus, overlay our all-too-human tendencies on the universal Spirit.

While it may seem to operate this way for some time in our development, eventually we begin to recognize that the Spirit is beyond the limitations imposed by our vital seekings. The higher aspirations and deeper meaning of our lives can at that point no longer be held hostage to the desire-soul's limited view.

Sri Aurobindo explains the transition to a new view of Karma, the spiritual view: "The universal Spirit in the law of Karma must deal with man in the lower scale of values only as a part of the transaction and as a concession to man's own present motives. Man himself puts these values, makes that demand for pleasure and prosperity and dreads their opposites, desires heaven more than he loves virtue, fears hell more than he abhors sin, and while he does so, the world-dispensation wears to him that meaning and colour."

This is however not the entire story: "The dependence of the pursuit of ethical values on a sanction by the inferior hedonistic values, material, vital and lower mental pleasure, pain and suffering, appeals strongly to our normal consciousness and will; but it ceases to have more than a subordinate force and finally loses all force as we grow towards greater heights of our being."

Sri Aurobindo reminds us that there is more to existence than our daily grasping and avoidance routines: "But the spirit of existence is not merely a legislator and judge concerned to maintain a standard of legal justice, to dole out deterrents and sanctions, rewards and penalties, ferocious pains of hell, indulgent joys of paradise. He is the Divine in the world, the Master of a spiritual evolution and the growing godhead in humanity."

As we transfer our view of the law of Karma to the larger evolutionary purpose of existence, we can begin "to develop a nobler spiritual law of Karma."

Sri Aurobindo, *Rebirth and Karma*, Section I, Chapter 12, Karma and Justice, pp. 106-107

A Higher Soul Nature and Law of Karma

While it is the first formulation of human motivation, the force of desire, attraction towards what is pleasant and avoidance of what is unpleasant, is not the sole motivating factor in our lives. We sometimes overrule physical and vital happiness to achieve results of another order. For instance, we may choose to forego the physical joys of food, sex or other pleasures in the pursuit of a mental or spiritual result. Similarly, many undergo extreme difficulties, privation and pain in order to achieve some goal, whether this be a goal of intellectual research or climbing mountains, or participation in extreme sports of various kinds. We see then, both the ability and the aspiration to move beyond the most basic law of attraction and repulsion, greed and fear, arising with the growth of the inherent powers that are our higher nature.

Sri Aurobindo discusses "our own greater motives of action". "The pursuit of Truth may entail on me penalties and sufferings; the service of my country or the world may demand from me loss of my outward happiness and good fortune or the destruction of my body; the increase of my strength of will and greatness of spirit may be only possible by the ardours of suffering and the firm renunciation of joys and pleasures."

This paradigm works not just in the present life but in whatever other lives the process of rebirth creates. "Happiness and sorrow, good fortune and ill-fortune are not my main concern whether in this birth or in future lives, but my perfection and the higher good of mankind purchased by whatever suffering and tribulation."

The joy that comes about through these acts is a higher spiritual joy, eventually leading to the "highest spiritual Ananda which has no dependence on outward circumstances, but rather is powerful to new-shape their meanings and transform their reactions. These things may be above the first formulation of the world energy here, may be influences from superior planes of the universal existence, but they are still a part of the economy of Karma here, a process of the spiritual evolution in the body. And they bring in a higher soul nature and will and action and consequence, a higher rule of Karma."

Once we admit the action of impulsions that defer the immediate seeking of joy or avoidance of pain, we develop a much more complex and subtle hierarchy of action and result of Karma.

Sri Aurobindo, *Rebirth and Karma*, Section I, Chapter 12, Karma and Justice, pp. 107-108

The Complex Web of Karma

When we think about the law of Karma, we tend to look at it from the ethical or moral implications. This leads us to question providence when we see evil apparently prospering and good apparently suffering. We then try to justify this obviously incorrect result with the idea that there was something in that person's past lives that justifies this "unjust" dispensation.

What we fail to consider is that different types of energy have different workings, and that to each type of energy the law of cause and effect provides its own type of result. To the strong belong the fruits of strength. If we reflect on it, dispassionately, without ethical preconceptions coloring our view, we would clearly find no grounds for disagreement. No one would expect that a person who embodies compassion or caring in their nature would be granted thereby a victory in the 100 meter dash in the Olympic Games. We naturally would expect that a trained athlete, focused on conditioning the body, and carrying out an intense programme of development of the physical capacity, would be the Olympic athlete.

Sri Aurobindo describes the interaction and relationship of these various types of energies, which in turn manifest based on stages, phases and appropriate times, to create a much more complete view of the working of the law of Karma, not as one immutable ethical or moral law, but as a subtle and highly complex standard which can actually provide us valuable insight as to the rationale for what are otherwise inexplicable results.

"If it is just that the virtuous man should be rewarded with success and happiness and the wicked man punished with downfall and pain at some time, in some life, on earth or in heaven or in hell, it is also just that the strong man should have the reward of his cultivated strength, the intellectual man the prize of his cultivated skill, the will that labours in whatever field the fruit of its effort and its works." This view transcends the ethical view.

"But what is right working in this connection of will and action and consequence? I may be religious and honest, but if I am dull, weak and incompetent? And I may be selfish and impious, but if I have the swift flame of intellect, the understanding brain, the skill to adapt means to ends, the firm courageous will fixed on its end? I have then an imperfection which must impose its consequences, but also I have powers which must make their way."

"The truth is that there are several orders of energy and their separate characteristic working must be seen, before their relations can be rightly discovered in the harmonies of Nature. A complex web is what we have to unravel. When we have seen the parts in the whole, the elements and their affinities in the mass, then only can we know the lines of Karma."

Sri Aurobindo, *Rebirth and Karma*, Section I, Chapter 12, Karma and Justice, pg. 108

SECTION II
THE LINES OF KARMA

CHAPTER THIRTEEN

THE FOUNDATION

Law of Nature and the Soul

To gain an understanding of the nature and action of the law of Karma, it is essential to distinguish the various elements involved. There is first, the law of Nature which expresses itself in the action of energy, of whatever type. Physicists tell us that for every action, there is an equal and opposite reaction; that is, that Energy functions under certain laws in the material world, and in fact is subject to calculation and the ability to be harnessed for work. We may explore the question of Energy further into the realm of life, mind and spirit, and similarly find laws of action and reaction that determine the movement and result of that energy.

A question arises whether this is purely a mechanical, external law of Nature to which the soul is subjected, in which case, as Sri Aurobindo points out "it cannot have a mental, moral and spiritual significance" ; or if Nature is "...not itself the energy, the work of a Mind, a Soul, a Spirit."

Next, the relationship of the soul to the action of Nature is a seminal concern for understanding the working of the law of Karma. "If the individual energy is that of a soul putting out action and receiving a return in kind, physical, mental, moral and spiritual from the universal energy, the universal energy too that makes the return should be that of an All-Soul in which and in relation to which this individual flame of the All-Soul lives." This is necessary if we see that the universal Energy carries any higher significance than just a physical law.

We observe that the individual expresses the energy of the universal, lives according to universal law, and carries out the force of the universal movement of energy. "But if that were all the truth, then there would be no real individual and no responsibility of any kind except the responsibility of universal Nature to carry out the idea or to execute the force put forth in the individual as in the universal by the All-Soul, the cosmic Spirit."

The individual acquires meaning and significance by virtue of its acting as an independent center of Energy capable of an individual response and return to the universal Energy. "But there is also this soul of the individual, and that is a being of the Infinite and a conscious and efficient portion of the All-Soul, a deputy or representative, and puts forth the energy given to it according to its own potentiality, type, limits with a will that is in some sense its own." It is the nexus caused by these two, the universal law of Nature and the reality of the individual soul, that provides us a platform for the action and meaning of the law of Karma.

Sri Aurobindo, *Rebirth and Karma*, Section II, Chapter 13, The Foundation, pg. 111

Individual Nature, Typal Nature and the Soul

Our individual nature and action represents a certain "uniqueness" within a larger framework of conformity to our "type" as a member of a species. Every species has what we may call a "typal" nature that provides a framework for the potentialities and development of each individual within that species. Thus, an ant will be seen to act in a way characteristic to ants, and this will be different than the way that a dog will act, although all dogs will act in a manner consistent with "dog-nature". Similarly all human beings share the basic characteristics of "human-nature".

Within this basic framework, however, individual human beings can express variances that provide an individuality to their representation of the human species.

The individual human being also embodies a soul which partakes of Divine Nature.

It is therefore the interaction of these three elements, the typal, the individual and the divine, that provides us the unique expression we recognize as a unique human being.

The concept of *Swabhava* expresses this idea that there is a "way of being" that is characteristic of each species and for each individual within the typal framework.

Sri Aurobindo describes the relation of *Swabhava* to *Swadharma*, the law of action of each being or type: "Man is at once himself, in a certain way peculiar and unique, and a depressed portion of God and a natural portion of mankind. There is in other words a general and an individual Swadharma or natural principle and law of all action for the kind and for the individual in the kind. And it is clear too that every action must be a particular application, a single result, a perfect or imperfect, right or perverted use of the general and within it of the individual swadharma."

"The law of the action is determined generally by this swabhava of the species and individually by the swabhava of the individual but within that larger circle."

Sri Aurobindo, *Rebirth and Karma*, Section II, Chapter 13, The Foundation, pg. 112

The Fundamental Meaning of Karma

The characteristic action of the typal formation, or even the individual action within the type, is not the entire picture of the universal manifestation. There is also the evolutionary power of the will of the Spirit that manifests through Nature. There is a continuous unfolding and development and this lends to the individual soul, as representative and portion of the Spirit, the ability to change. While the action of Karma, as a law of energy in Nature, will bring results forward, the individual soul has the choice of action, reaction, response and development that can make an enormous difference over time in the ongoing process.

Sri Aurobindo describes this process: "His nature is what it is because he has so made it by his past; he has induced this present formulation by a precedent will in his spirit."

"He has developed by his own long evolution of that humanity the character and law of action of his present individual being; he has built his own height and form of human nature. He may change what he has made, he may rise even, if that be within the possibilities of the universe, beyond human and to or towards superhuman nature."

The result of past action, in the form of the present karmic circumstance the individual must experience, creates tendencies and, for an evolutionary process, obstacles to change. However, these obstacles can become opportunities for the conscious exercise of the will of the Spirit to modify results going forward and create a different formation than the one that would otherwise project itself forward in a static circumstance.

"This evolution and all its circumstances, his life, its form, its events, its values arise out of that urge and are shaped according to the past, present or future active will of his spirit. As is his use of the energy, so was and will be the return of the universal energy to him now and hereafter. This is the fundamental meaning of Karma."

Sri Aurobindo, *Rebirth and Karma*, Section II, Chapter 13, The Foundation, pp. 112-113

A Complex Interaction of Energies

The complex nature of the lines of Karma is in part due to the fact that there are numerous different forms and types of energy at work which each have their own separate working, impulsion and direction. These different forms of energy interact with one another and modify the pure action of the others so that the eventual result is mixed and diluted.

Sri Aurobindo describes the different types of energies: "There is in the world of birth an energy of physical being and nature, arising out of the physical an energy of vital being and nature, arising out of the vital an energy of mental being and nature, arising out of the mental an energy of spiritual or supramental being and nature. And each of these forms of energy has a law of its own, lines of its own action, a right to its own manner or operation and existence, because each is fundamental to some necessity of the whole. And we see accordingly that each in its impulse follows its own lines regardless of the rest, each in the combination imposes as much of its domination as it can on the others."

Within each type of energy, too, there are sub-types. "The mental being is itself a most complex thing and has several forms of energy, an intellectual, a moral, an emotional, a hedonistic energy of mental nature, and the will in each is in itself absolute for its own rule and is yet forced to be modified in action by the running into it and across it of the other strands."

The interaction and inter-relationship of all these different forms of energy creates a complex web of action that cannot be fully defined by any one specific term. We must be able to take account of vital attraction, physical action, as well as intellectual and emotional drives when we try to understand the full working of the law of "cause and effect". It would only be from a consciousness that views and reconciles the entire complexity of the creation that we could hope to develop a complete understanding. Until that time, we must appreciate the fact that no one drive or impulsion can act uninfluenced and unimpeded by other drives, influences or powers of action.

Sri Aurobindo, *Rebirth and Karma*, Section II, Chapter 13, The Foundation, pp. 113-114

Moral Law Is Not the Sole
Significance of the Universal Manifestation

When we consider the law of Karma, the first thought is that it is some kind of moral or ethical framework for the universe. It is much simpler to try to understand our lives and the significance of life itself if we can find a way to boil it down to one dominant concept or principle. The reality, however, is far more complex than such an approach can actually resolve.

Sri Aurobindo comments on this issue: "The universe is not solely an ethical proposition, a problem of the antinomy of the good and the evil; the Spirit of the universe can in no way be imagined as a rigid moralist concerned only with making all things obey the law of moral good, or a stream of tendency towards righteousness attempting, hitherto with only a very poor success, to prevail and rule, or a stern Justicer rewarding and punishing creatures in a world that he has made or has suffered to be full of wickedness and suffering and evil."

A serious review of the many-sided and multifarious manifestation in the universe makes it patently obvious that there are a variety of goals and principles at work, interacting and in some cases actually appearing to be in conflict with one another. We can even determine a hierarchy which helps us resolve apparent contradictions with the advent of a new power or term that needs to modify and upgrade the action of a prior line of development.

"The law of the world is not this alone that our good brings good to us and our evil brings evil, nor is its sufficient key the ethical-hedonistic rule that our moral good brings to us happiness and success and our moral evil brings to us sorrow and misfortune."

We need to expand our view and understanding of the development of the universal manifestation to get a true sense of what the real goals and principles are. We can say that the moral and ethical law appears to be one, among a number of other principles, that has a role in the human development. This law, however, is constrained and modified by other principles and powers that need to be taken into account.

Sri Aurobindo, *Rebirth and Karma*, Section II, Chapter 13, The Foundation, pg. 114

Basic Principle of the Law of Karma

It is clear that we cannot encompass the entire complexity of the universe and the various forces at work within a definition of a law of Karma that fixates solely on an ethical or moral code of recompense or retribution. And yet it is also quite clear that there are certain laws operative in the universe that show that there is Intelligence at work. Each type of energy has its own pattern of action. In the physical world, we see that scientists have formulated physical energy laws under the principle "for every action there is an equal and opposite reaction." If we examine emotional energy, mental energy, ethical or moral energy, we find that there are corollary results that indicate that while the type of energy at work is different, and therefore the exact manner of its working varies, there is nevertheless a system of output of energy leading to a characteristic result.

Sri Aurobindo asks us to begin our understanding of the law of Karma by creating a formulation that is its most simple and universal principle, and to then utilize this basic principle as a foundational step for our deeper review and understanding of the action of Karma:

"And for a beginning it is best to phrase the law of Karma as generally and vaguely as may be and put it simply thus without any particular colour or content that according to the energy put forth shall be its return, not with any mathematical precision of conscious will and its mechanical consequences, but subject to the complicated working of any world forces."

He goes on to clarify further: "The whole law of the cosmic action or even the one law governing all the others cannot well be the measure of a physical, mechanical and chemical energy, nor the law of a life force, nor a moral law or law of mind or of idea forces; for it is evident that none of these things by its single self covers or accounts for all the fundamental powers."

Sri Aurobindo, *Rebirth and Karma*, Section II, Chapter 13, The Foundation, pp. 114-115

Unraveling the Complexity
of the Law of Action and Reaction

All energy moves, acts and has its effects in a field of activity. We need to review various factors to understand this action and the resultant effects. Some of the factors include:

1. type of energy. different types of energy work in different ways wth varying objects, according to the principle of action of that type of energy. Physical energy may build up mountains or flatten buildings. Vital energy brings about life and growth. Emotional, intellectual or other mental forms of energy each have their own respective impacts. One cannot expect an emotional energy to build up mountains! At the same time, energies of one type can and do have potential impacts at numerous levels. Thus, a tornado, in flattening a community, can bring about intense emotional suffering in the residents affected, although it does not, of itself, have an emotional aspect to it. With respect to human action, the actual energy released is generally of a mixed, not single, type and thus leads to mixed results.

2. intensity of the energy. a weak energy has very little ability to create strong effects or results.

3. the field of action of the energy. the operative conditions surrounding the action of the energy influence the potential impact and results, as well as where and how it is going into action.

4. countervailing or offsetting energies at work. in the world at large, no energy works purely in its own native action; rather, it's action is modified and influenced by other forces at work at the same time.

5. receptivity of the object to the type of energy being applied. The more receptivity of the object, the more effective the action of the force at work, generally.

These factors help us to understand the complexity of the action of the law of Karma. It is not simply a mechanical rule of "action/reaction" but rather, a resultant impact taking into account the many factors that influence the action. We also tend to fixate on the law of Karma as something that affects the individual expressing the action, and while that is true, it is not the entire story. There is an effect on the universal manifestation, the others with whom we interact and the long-term spiritual goals of the manifestation.

Sri Aurobindo discusses these issues at length, including the following summary: "The nature of the energies we put forth and even the return and reflex of their consequence upon us affects not only ourselves but all around us and we must account too for the direction of our acts upon others, its effect upon them and the return of the direction and rebound of consequence of the effect upon our own life and being. But the energy we put forth on others is ordinarily of a mixed character, physical, vital, moral, mental and spiritual, and the return and consequence too are of a mixed character. A physical action, a vital pressure thrown forth from ourselves carries in it a mental or moral as well as a physical and vital power and issues often quite beyond our conscious will and knowledge and the consequence to ourselves and to others is found to be different enough in character and measure from anything we intended or could have calculated and foreseen."

Sri Aurobindo, *Rebirth and Karma*, Section II, Chapter 13, The Foundation, pp. 115-116

The Three Inter-Connected Aspects of the Law of Karma

All existence is a nexus between the individual, the universal and the transcendent. The law of Karma, therefore, in order to be fully understood, must take into account each of these three aspects. Most people look at the law of Karma from a purely individual standpoint. This obviously is too simplistic a view and does not provide much guidance or real understanding. It is just one aspect and not the complete picture. The idea that a person is reborn from life to life with a consistent personality that is subject to some kind of retributive justice is clearly not the meaning of the law of Karma.

We have explored the interaction of the individual and the society and world within which the individual lives and acts and determined that part of the action of Karma is the impact of the individual on the world and the world on the individual. The individual as a manifestation of the universal force of Nature expresses larger forces that are a work generally and which have consequences generally. This too, however, does not present us a complete picture.

In order to complete the view we need to remind ourselves that the ultimate significance of our lives lies in the connection to the transcendent Spirit which is manifesting itself through Time using both the individual and the universal as the field of that manifestation.

Sri Aurobindo integrates these three together: "But there is another, an ultimate and essential sense of Karma, a relation in it between the soul in us and the Supreme or the All-Self; on that all is founded and to that all leads and must refer to it at every step. That relation too is not so simple a thing as is imagined by the religions. For it must answer to a very vast spiritual sense underlying the whole process of Karma and there must be a connection of each of our workings in the use of the universal energy to that fundamental and perhaps infinite significance. These three things, the will of the soul in Nature and the action of Nature in and on the soul and through it and back to it, the effect of the intercrossing between the action of the soul on others and the return to it of the force of its action complicated by theirs, and the meaning of the soul's action in relation to its own highest Self and the All-Self, to God, make up between them all the bearings of Karma."

Sri Aurobindo, *Rebirth and Karma*, Section II, Chapter 13, The Foundation, pg. 116

CHAPTER FOURTEEN

THE TERRESTRIAL LAW

Failure of the Ordinary View of Karma

We generally approach the world and life with an overlay of the moral and ethical viewpoint that we would like to see operative there. We tend to try to shape the world in our own image, rather than try to view it "as it is" independent of our specific viewpoint or ideology. This filtering of experience, however, tends to distort the reality and eventually, to mislead us about the significance of our lives. Sri Aurobindo points out that "The problem of knowledge is after all this, to reflect the movements of the Infinite and see, and not to force it into a mould prepared for it by our intelligence."

This faulty methodology of knowledge colors our view of Karma as well. We expect the world to conform to our notions of morality, right and wrong, and when we see that the world appears not to reward the good, or punish the evil, we try to find a way to justify what we perceive to be a failure of the universe by creating the idea of rewards or punishments in some after-life or next lifetime.

A more sound method must be used to understand the significance of life and the world, a method not colored by emotional or mental preconceptions, a method that first observes, then organizes the observed facts before overlaying convenient interpretations over them.

Sri Aurobindo proposes in this chapter to do such a review of terrestrial life, as a basis and foundation for a further review of the concept of Karma.

Sri Aurobindo, *Rebirth and Karma*, Section II, Chapter 14, The Terrestrial Law, pg. 117

Moral Law and Terrestrial Existence

Perhaps the must perplexing and frustrating set of facts that compels our attention revolves around the inter-relationship of good and evil in the world. It is obvious that good acts sometimes bring about evil results; and that things we consider to be evil can eventually yield good results. This is not meant to justify "doing evil for the sake of good" or abandoning good since it can lead to evil; rather, it is intended to provide us insight into the larger working of the universal manifestation that apparently does not have moral results as its sole goal.

Sri Aurobindo describes this issue: "The difficulty remains why that good should use evil as one and almost the chief of its means or the dominant moral law, sovereign, unescapable, categorical, imperative, the practical governor, if not the reason of our existence, should be compelled to fulfil itself through so much that is immoral and by the agency of a non-moral force, through hell on earth and hell beyond, through petty cruelty of punishment and huge fury of avenging calamity, through an immeasurable and, as it seems, never ending sequence of pain and suffering and torture."

The conclusion is obvious when we remove the artificial filters from our vision: "It must surely be because there are other things in the Infinite and therefore other laws and forces here and of these the moral law, however great and sovereign to itself, has to take account and is compelled to accommodate its own lines to their curve of movement."

If this is the case, then in order to get a clearer picture of the action of the moral law and its relation to our existence and the question of rebirth, we need to first gain an understanding of those other forces that impact, modify, dilute or derail the pure action of the moral law.

Sri Aurobindo, *Rebirth and Karma*, Section II, Chapter 14, The Terrestrial Law, pg. 118

The Terrestrial Law of Physical Energy

In our ongoing attempt to infuse moral significance into everything that happens in the world, we frequently imply that events and forces occurring in the physical world are "God's retribution" for some failing on someone's part. In this view, tornadoes, floods, earthquakes are a sign of some higher judgment upon us. Victims then cry that they do not know why "God did this to them", or why the innocent children caught in the maelstrom were made to suffer.

Sri Aurobindo makes the point that when we remove this moral filter from our view, it becomes clear that the physical energy operates on its own principles and that it is not some kind of concious retributive machinery of God. "The flood" or "Sodom and Gomorrah" do not represent God's judgment on humanity, but results of physical energy carrying out its natural functions regardless of who or what happens to be in the way. "The fire is no respecter of persons and if the saint or the thinker is cast into it, it will not spare his body. The sea, the stormwind, the rock on which the ship drives do not ask whether the just man drowned in the waters deserved his fate. If the lightning that strikes impartially tree or beast or man, is–but it would appear in the case of the man alone, for the rest is accident,–the sword of God or the instrument of Karma, if the destruction wrought by the volcano, the typhoon or the earthquake is a punishment for the sins of the community or individually of the sins in a past life of each man there that suffers or perishes, at least the natural forces know it not and care nothing about it and rather they conceal from us in the blind impartiality of their rage all evidence of any such intention. The sun shines and the rain falls on the just and the unjust alike; the beneficence and the maleficence of Nature, the gracious and dreadful Mother, her beauty and terror, her utility and her danger are bestowed and inflicted without favour or disfavour on all her children and the good man is no more her favourite than the sinner. If a law of moral punishment is imposed through the action of her physical forces, it must be by a Will from above her or a Force acting unknown to her in her inconscient bosom."

These physical forces would otherwise be a blunt and indiscriminate instrument that strikes down whole communities to target one person. Certainly a moral justicer would use a finer tool to target just those who need to be targeted without involving vast numbers of others, including innocent beings, plants and animals in the destruction.

Sri Aurobindo, *Rebirth and Karma*, Section II, Chapter 14, The Terrestrial Law, pp. 118-119

Physical Energy and Moral Retribution

Having excluded the possibility that physical energy consciously conducts a policy of reward and punishment, there is still the possibility that physical energy carries out such a policy directed or guided by some conscious intelligence above or beyond that utilizes it. Sri Aurobindo describes what this would imply: "If a law of moral punishment is imposed through the action of her physical forces, it must be by a Will from above her or a Force acting unknown to her in her inconscient bosom."

The implications of this approach however are that we then create a vision of deity that would be more terrible than the worst human rulers we could imagine, as Sri Aurobindo explains: "But such a Will could not be itself that of a moral Being ethical after the conceptions of man,–unless indeed it resembled man in his most coldly pitiless and savage moral reason or unreason. For its action involves terrors of punishment that would be abhorred as atrocities in an all-powerful human ruler and could not be other than monstrous in a moral Divine Ruler. A personal God so acting would be a Jehovah-Moloch, a merciless and unrighteous demander of righteousness and mercy."

It is true that we have seen some religions actually embrace such a vision at various points in human history. At the same time, the human spirit refuses to accept that this is the ultimate truth of the world. The idea that individual human moral failure unleashes powerful, indiscriminate physical forces to rain down death, suffering and destruction on large masses of humanity, along with the rest of the creatures in existence, the good and the evil, the innocent and the guilty, is abhorrent to our intuitive sense of significance in our lives and in the world. We sometimes rail against disaster by asking why God would take the lives of innocent children or why God would unleash the fire, whirlwind or tempest on simple people living innocuous lives.

We are left then to infer that physical nature operates under its own rules under a non-moral framework and that morality only enters in when we can see the action of mind and intelligent directed action. There are many powers at work in the world. They interact and impact one another, some providing the physical framework for conscious life and existence and others developing higher powers of insight, understanding, moral and ethical development within that framework and its limitations and conditions.

Sri Aurobindo, *Rebirth and Karma*, Section II, Chapter 14, The Terrestrial Law, pp. 119-120

Each Energy Carries Out Its Own Function

In the Kena Upanishad, the seer describes the various physical forces, the force of fire, the force of wind and their characteristic power of action. Fire is the force that burns all created things. Wind is the force that moves all created things. Agni, the God of Fire, replied when asked about his power: "Even all this I could burn, all that is upon the earth."

We have an intuitive sense of a moral law existing in the Universe, and this provides us a clue that there is such a component in the manifestation; however, it operates under what Sri Aurobindo elsewhere calls "the logic of the Infinite" and is not limited by the circumscribed human view that we try to overlay on the universe.

Everywhere we turn we find that the creation is far more complex, inter-related and consisting of symbiotic parts and movements, than anything that our human mind can create. We cannot therefore hope to judge the creation in its entirety using that limited consciousness.

Sri Aurobindo provides a clear explanation of this difference in consciousness: "All her constructions and motions are those of an illimitable intuitive wisdom too great and spontaneous and mysteriously self-effective to be described as an intelligence, of a Power and Will working for Time in eternity with an inevitable and forecasting movement in each of its steps, even in those steps that in their outward or superficial impetus seem to us inconscient. And as there is in her this greater consciousness and greater power, so too there is an illimitable spirit of harmony and beauty in her constructions that never fails her, though its works are not limited by our aesthetic canons. An infinite hedonism too is there, an illimitable spirit of delight, of which we become aware when we enter into impersonal unity with her; and even as that in her which is terrible is a part of her beauty, that in her which is dangerous, cruel, destructive is a part of her delight, her universal Ananda."

No human limited mental consciousness is able to grasp the immensity, power, complexity or purposes of that larger consciousness. Similarly the moral sense has its own validation if viewed from the larger view of the Infinite, even if it confounds our mental idea of morality.

"The physical law is the right and justice, the duty, the ought of the physical world." Each thing "observes the lines of its physical energy and is concerned with no other law or justice. No law of Karma, the moral law included, could exist, if there were not to begin with this principle as the first foundation of order."

Sri Aurobindo, *Rebirth and Karma*, Section II, Chapter 14, The Terrestrial Law, pg. 120

And *The Upanishads*, Kena Upanishad, pp. 104-105

Transcending Physical Nature

As human beings we not only experience physical nature, in ourselves and in the world around us, but we also incorporate vital powers and a mental and spiritual nature. These additional forces confront physical nature and seek to go beyond the limitations imposed by it. Sri Aurobindo describes the role of man in the world: "...as a soul evolving the power of consciousness secret in her, his business is to know and to use her law and even in knowing and using it to transcend her more material limit, habit, purpose and formula. Observance of Nature but also transcendence of first nature is continually the purpose of the Spirit within him."

Evolution, both on the physical plane and as a process that introduces new principles into the world action, principles of life, mind and spirit, represents this attempt of Nature to exceed its current formulation and to manifest something new, more powerful, with greater powers of consciousness at play.

The role of man in this process is to interject a conscious actor in the process of evolution and transcendence. "Man meets with the powers of his mind the rule of the physical action and the law of vital Karma, brings in a law of mental and moral Karma and lifts along the ladder of these scales to something more, to a potency of spiritual action which may even lead him to an exceeding of Karma itself, a freedom from or of birth and becoming, a perfecting transcendence."

While physical nature continues to carry out the law of its action, we begin to see opportunities to respond consciously, to resist, modify, enhance or leave behind the purely physical and mechanical action of Nature and this brings about new possibilities along with a new level of complexity in the interaction.

Sri Aurobindo, *Rebirth and Karma*, Section II, Chapter 14, The Terrestrial Law, pg. 121

Challenging the Limitations of Physical Nature

There is a story stemming from the Greek tradition which illustrates the role of man in physical nature–The story of Prometheus. The name itself stems from Greek roots that mean "forethinker". The story goes that the Gods were withholding the power of fire from humanity. The allusion however widens to represent powers of understanding, progress and mastery over the forces of physical nature that enter into the world with the advent of human-embodied powers of creativity and originality and the corresponding application of the powers of mind and will to manifest what was formerly latent in Nature, in most cases against intense opposition (in the original story Zeus, king of the Gods opposed the action of Prometheus and penalized him with constant and ever-recurring pain and anguish). Zeus also created Pandora and gave her the famous "Pandora's box" in retribution for the action of Prometheus. The symbolism of Pandora's box represents all the "unintended consequences" that arise from the forward seeking mind of humanity attempting to understand, master and develop beyond the limits of physical nature.

This story illustrates the struggle of man to escape the control of the forces of Nature. Sri Aurobindo describes this process: "He defies her powers, transgresses her limitations, sins constantly against her first prohibitions, takes her punishments and overcomes them, becomes by wrestling of his mind and will with her acquainted with her greater possibilities which she herself has left unused while she waited for his coming. She meets his effort with physical obstruction and opposition, with a No that constantly recedes, with the mask of his own ignorance, with the menace of her danger."

The seeking for a moral law in the world is an attempt to understand a higher order or organization than the purely non-moral physical forces clashing and building. The manifestation of life, and later of mind, upsets the established order of action of the purely physical forces of Nature, and seeks to bring about a new and higher order based on the increased complexity of this new, higher expression of consciousness in the world.

The story of Prometheus is an allusion that has gripped the mind of man for ages, from the time of Aeschylus and his play "Prometheus Bound", to the time of Shelley and his poem "Prometheus Unbound". We see around us the tremendous development of new powers as we explore every aspect of physical Nature, and we see at the same time the enormous unintended consequences and both individual and collective suffering entailed in exceeding the original limitations placed upon us. We see here that Prometheus, the forethinker, represents the evolutionary process to bring about the expansion of consciousness in the world.

Sri Aurobindo, *Rebirth and Karma*, Section II, Chapter 14, The Terrestrial Law, pp. 121-122

The Will To Mastery Over Physical Nature

Physical Nature is non-moral in its response to the efforts of humanity. This means that it will provide a commensurate energy response to the effort made to utilize or harness its forces, based solely on the energy and not on some concept of moral or ethical right or wrong. The law of Karma on the physical plane is essentially a law of "cause and effect."

Sri Aurobindo describes this relationship: "But in fact all that the godhead of physical Nature is concerned with in man's dealings with her is to observe a just law of return of her energies to his effort. Wherever his knowledge and will can harmonise itself with the lines of her energies, she makes a return according to its action on her: where it works on her with insufficiency, ignorance, carelessness, error, she overwhelms his effort or injures; as he wills more and discovers more, she returns to him a greater utility and fruit of her powers, consents to his masteries and favours his violences."

We can witness this process at work in the events of the last 200 years. An increasing concentration and focus on the elemental powers of physical Nature has led to discoveries that could only seem miraculous to human beings of earlier centuries. Today we take it for granted that we can observe actions in distant parts of the globe through satellite, television and internet; communicate with virtually any part of the world via wireless cell phones; fly through the air at supersonic speeds; travel into outer space; unlock enormous energies through splitting of the atom; harness the power of the sun through solar energy; transplant organs from one human being to another; and modify the very genetic structure of living beings. Each of these developments, representative of the type of will to mastery over physical Nature that we have seen develop during this time, has dramatically increased the power of action and base of knowledge of humanity, but none of them has been without their down-side consequences, some of which threaten the continued existence of all life on the planet, such as destructive nuclear weapons; global climate change, world-wide chemical contamination of the air, soil and water; and unforeseen consequences of genetic tampering.

Sri Aurobindo anticipated this type of much wider responsiveness of Nature to human development of knowledge and will: "There are indications that by a more direct pressure of a mental and psychical energy on the physical, the response can be made more variable, the physical depart from what seem to be fixed limits and habits, and it is conceivable that as knowledge and will entered into the region of higher and yet higher powers, the action of physical energy might grow entirely responsive, giving whatever return is seemingly demanded from her, and its lines perfectly flexible. But even this transcendence would have to regard the great original measures fixed by the All-Will: there could be a free use, perhaps a large transformation of the physical energy, but not a departure from its fundamental law and purpose."

Sri Aurobindo, *Rebirth and Karma*, Section II, Chapter 14, The Terrestrial Law, pp. 122-123

Physical Nature Is Non-Moral and Non-Ethical In Its Results

As we have been examining physical Nature and its forces, it has become obvious that the return or response of the energy, the essence of the law of "cause and effect" which underlies or notion of Karma, is strictly in line with our adherence to the principles and laws of the physical universe and does not include any moral or ethical component. Physical Nature will put into our hands the power to split the atom if we focus intensely enough, regardless of whether we will use it benignly or malignantly.

We try to impugn an ethical motive in the results of physical energy, but in the purest sense, physical energy simply does not have this impulsion. The concept of Karma that includes a "payback" in terms of morality or ethics is actually something that arises with the development of higher forms of consciousness.

Sri Aurobindo describes the response of Nature: "Physical Nature gives impartially her results and rewards and demands from man observance not of the moral but the physical law: she asks for a just knowledge and a scrupulous practice of her physical lines and nothing else. There is no karmic retort from her on the many cruelties of science, no revolt against an unethical use of her facilities, much punishment of ignorance but none of wickedness."

"Man may and does invent cruel and immoral means of getting at physical knowledge and its powers or turn to unethical ends the energies she places at his service, but that is a matter between his will and his own soul and of his relation with other living beings, his and their concern and not hers."

Sri Aurobindo points out that with the entry of the life energy into physical Nature, we begin to see the first inklings of some kind of energetic response that begins to take into account the effect on life, with the possibility of a response that goes beyond the strictly physical energies to balance excesses, but even here, it is not a moral or ethical principle, but some other life-basis that determines the actual reaction.

Sri Aurobindo, *Rebirth and Karma,* Section II, Chapter 14, The Terrestrial Law, pg. 123

The Vital Life Energy In Creation Is Non-Moral and Non-Ethical

As we turn our attention from the physical energies of the manifestation to the vital energies of life, it becomes once again quite obvious that there is a law of energy here that has its own rule and precision, but that this is not a "moral" or "ethical" law of action.

Sri Aurobindo reviews the functioning of the life energy: "The fundamental right and justice of life is to follow the curve of the vital energies, to maintain the functions of the life force and to give a return to its own powers. Its function is to survive, to reproduce itself, to grow and possess and enjoy, to prolong and enlarge and assure its action, power, having, pleasure as much as earth will allow. All means are good to life that secure these ends: the rest is a matter of right balance between the vital energy and its physical means, of a putting forth of its powers and the kind of return it gets for those powers."

The means used by the life energy to effect its ends makes it quite clear that it is not "moral" in the sense that humanity judges that concept: "Death is her second means of self-preservation, destruction her constant instrument for change and renovation and progress, suffering inflicted on oneself or on others oftenest her price for victory and pleasure. All life lives upon other life, makes a place for itself by encroachment and exploitation, possesses by association but even more by struggle. Life acts by mutual shock and mutual use of creatures by each other; but it works only partly by mutual help and very much by a mutual assault and devouring."

The vital force operates on a different law of action than the physical force of the universe, but it also represents a truth of the manifestation: "...we find in it a mysteriously perfect order, the work of a deep and illimitable intuitive wisdom, an immense Power and will at its perfectly seeing work, a great whole of beauty and harmony built out of what seems to us a system of discords, a might joy of life and creation which no heaviest toll of individual death or suffering can tire or discourage and which, when we enter into oneness with the great Ananda of its movement, these things seem rather to cast into relief and against the hue of its ecstasy these shades not to matter."

Sri Aurobindo, *Rebirth and Karma*, Section II, Chapter 14, The Terrestrial Law, pp. 123-124

The Dharma of the Vital Life Nature

With the advent of the vital life force into the world we see what some have called "the law of the jungle" and others "survival of the fittest" as the basic principle of the life energy. Even for human beings, we start from this basis and only add ethical and moral considerations later as mind-nature begins to develop and make itself felt in transcending the basic instincts of the vital force.

Sri Aurobindo comments on the nature of the vital power in its action in the world: "At first he is compelled to obey its instincts and has to act even as the animal, but in the enlarged terms of a mentalised impulsion and an increasingly clear consciousness and responsible will in what he does. He too has first to strive to exist, to make a place for himself and his kind, to grow and possess and enjoy, to prolong, to enlarge and assure the first vital lines of his life movement. He to does it even as the others, by battle and slaughter, by devouring, by encroachment, by laying his yoke on earth and her products and on her brute children and on his fellowmen. His virtue, his dharma of the vital nature, *virtus, arete,* is first an obligation to strength and swiftness and courage and all things that make for survival, mastery and success."

The rule of return on energy is operative here by providing results based on the ability to harness and master the powers of the vital force. There may be an element of self-control, discipline or focus of energy, but these are implementations of the law of vital force and their goal, and their result, is to enhance the success of the vital life nature.

Sri Aurobindo, *Rebirth and Karma*, Section II, Chapter 14, The Terrestrial Law, pp. 124-125

Dynamic Life Action and Karma

Sri Aurobindo summarizes the action of the life energy and its results: "The battle in life's primitive values is to the strong and the race to the swift, and the weak and the torpid cannot claim the goal and the crown on the strength of their greater virtue; and there is in this a justice, while the moral principle of reward would be here an injustice, for it would be a denial of the principle of the right returns of energy which is fundamental to any possible law of Karma."

When we begin to go beyond the raw energy of the life force by bringing in mental intelligence and will, we still have not overturned the basic and essential goal of the life energy; rather, we simply enhance the potential results through a more powerful and effective action. "Raise the action by the powers of the mind and still the greater successes, the glory and the victory, fall to the men of great intelligence and the men of great will and not necessarily to the more ethical intelligence or to the more moralised will. Morality counts in this dynamic aspect of life only as a prudential check or a concentrating tapasya. Life helps those who most wisely and faithfully follow her impulses while observing her limits and restraints or those who most powerfully aid her greater impulses of expansion."

The essence of the law of Karma is "cause and effect", so one would expect, when removing the artificial "ethical filter" from our vision, to find that at each level, physical energy, or vital energy, there would appear a consistency and a pattern of action that returns the result based on the energy that is put forth.

The first drives of the human being involve harnessing our basic mental capacities and dynamic will to the aggrandisement and satisfaction of our vital impulses and needs–to survive and thrive in the world and achieve the fruits of our desires and action.

Sri Aurobindo, *Rebirth and Karma*, Section II, Chapter 14, The Terrestrial Law, pg. 125

Transcending the Vital Life Nature

With the advent of mentality in our lives, we begin to devise strategies to deal with the issues raised by the vital nature. We remain, for the most part, under the control of the impulses of the vital nature, under the control of desire in all its forms. Some seek for security through attempting a path through life that understands the framework of the vital force and tries to stay within its limits; however, most of us are primarily driven by the need to expand, to grow, to exceed prior limits and this obviously increases both the opportunities and the risks of the lives we lead.

Sri Aurobindo discusses this issue: "He is avid of experience, of the unmeasured and unknown in power and experience and enjoyment as of the common and known and safe, of the perilous extremes as of the sane averages. He must sound all life's possibilities, test the wrong as well as the right use of her energies, pay his toll of suffering and get his prize of more splendid victories."

The mind's role in all of this drama of the life force has been to aid in both the drive towards stability and security and to assist in the drive toward expansion and new experience. The primary goal has been driven by the vital force's impulsion.

It is possible, however, as the mental force becomes more certain in its manifestation, that a new balance can be reached where the mind actual begins to uplift and guide, and to provide new direction, control and motives for the vital energy. "It is only by a transformation of our inner life that we can get beyond the magnified, mentalised, reasoning and consciously willing animal that for the most part the greater number of us are and only by raising it up to unity with some spiritual power we have not yet reached that we can hope to transform vital nature and make her a free instrument of the higher spirit. Then man may be really what he strives to be, master of his life, in control of vital and physical Nature."

"Meanwhile it is through an inward turn of his mind that he gets to something like a transcendence, a living not for life but for truth, for beauty, for power of the soul, for good and right, love, justice. It is this endeavour that brings down ito the lower rounds of energy the powers of a higher circle, something of a mental and a truly moral tending at its end to become a spiritual law of action and the fruits of action of Karma."

Sri Aurobindo, *Rebirth and Karma*, Section II, Chapter 14, The Terrestrial Law, pp. 125-126

CHAPTER FIFTEEN

MIND NATURE AND LAW OF KARMA

Man, the Mental Being

In our review of physical nature and vital nature, we have found a non-moral action that follows the lines set down for the working of physical forces and vital forces. The first stirrings of mental force are harnessed to the vital fulfillment. If this were the entirety of our capabilities, we would have found a simple, dynamic law of existence, that would have excluded just about everything that we consider to be distinctly human. Because in the end, despite the focus we put into physical and vital actions, the one central reality that is most characteristic for humanity is our embodiment of mentality and the principles that this brings into life.

Sri Aurobindo integrates the mental principle into our view of human nature: "Man is not after all in the essence of his manhood or in the inner reality of his soul a vital and physical being raised to a certain power of mental will and intelligence."

"But the more he looks into himself and the more he goes inward and lives intimately and preeminently in his mind and soul, the more he discovers that he is in his essential nature a mental being encased in body and enmeshed in the life activities, *manu, manomaya purusha*. He is more than a thinking, willing and feeling result of the mechanism of the physical or an understanding nexus of the vital forces. There is a mental energy of his being that overtops, pervades and utilises the terrestrial action and his own terrestrial nature."

The entry of the mental force into the world brings with it another line of energy that has its own laws of action and reaction, and thus, we add in the impact of the mind's forces to our understanding of the law of Karma.

Sri Aurobindo, *Rebirth and Karma*, Section II, Chapter 15, Mind Nature and Law of Karma, pg. 127

The Multiple Strands of the Mental Being

Before we begin our review of the lines of Karma related to the mental being, it is essential to gain a clear perspective on the various aspects that make up our mental functioning. There is the practical mind that involves itself with the physical and vital levels of existence and works to manage and utilize them to best advantage; there is also a higher mind of thought and concept, as well as an aesthetic and an emotional aspect that weave the complex fabric that we consider to be mental functioning.

Sri Aurobindo explains: "The mental energy divides itself and runs in many directions, has an ascending scale of the levels of its action, a great variety and combination of its dynamic aims and purposes. There are many strands of its weaving and it follows each along its own line and combines manifoldly he threads of one with the threads of another. There is in it an energy of thought that puts itself out for a return and a constant increase of knowledge, an energy of will that casts itself forth for a return and increase of conscious mastery, fulfilment of the being, execution of will in action, an energy of conscious aesthesis that feels out for a return and an increase of the creation and enjoyment of beauty, an energy of emotion that demands in its action a return and a constant increase of the enjoyment and satisfaction of the emotional power of the being. All these energies act in a way for themselves and yet depend upon and are inextricably accompanied and mingled with each other. At the same time mind has descended into matter and has to act in and through this world of the vital and physical energy and to consent to and make something of the lines of the vital and physical Karma."

It is not simply the complexity of these different energies and levels of action that we have to contend with; we also have to take into account the varying concentration and intensity of the energy put forth within each of these lines. A weak force will soon be deflected, drowned out or watered down by the myriad other active forces around it and with which it needs to contend.

Sri Aurobindo, *Rebirth and Karma*, Section II, Chapter 15, Mind Nature and Law of Karma, pp. 127-128

The Evolution of the Mental Power and Its Manifestation

It is man's destiny to represent and carry out the establishment of the force of mentality into the world, as man is characteristically a mental being. While the mental power takes up and thereby influences and modifies the action of physical forces and vital forces, the essence of mentality can be seen when we exercise the truly mental powers, independent of their specific impact on physicality and vitality.

Sri Aurobindo discusses this: "There is a higher law of mental being and nature of which he is bound to become aware and to seek to impose it on his life and his action. At first he is very predominantly governed by the life needs and the movement of the life energies, and it is in applying his mental energy to them and to the world around him that he makes the earliest development of his powers of knowledge and will and trains the crude impulses that lead him into the path of his emotional, aesthetic and moral evolution. But always there is a certain obscure element that takes pleasure in the action of the mental energies for their own sake and it is this, however imperfect at first in self-consciousness and intelligence, that represents the characteristic intention of Nature in him and makes his mental and eventually his spiritual evolution inevitable."

The initial preoccupation with the physical and vital levels, to satisfy the needs, desires and demands of life, focused on survival, enjoyment, growth and success in life, seems to be the primary function carried out by the mind. This viewpoint dismisses or devalues the "seeking for knowledge, mastery, beauty, a purer emotional delight for their own sake...."

"But the finer and more developed mind in humanity has always turned towards an opposite self-seeing, inclined to regard this as the most characteristic and valuable element of our being and been ready to sacrifice much and sometimes all to its calls or its imperative mandate."

This represents a reversal of seeing that takes the animal being out of the center of our universe and reorients our viewpoint toward the longer evolutionary cycles and the systematic development of higher forms of energy in the successive manifestation. "Then life itself would be in reality for man only a field of action for the evolution, the opportunity of new experience, the condition of difficult effort and mastery of the mental and spiritual being."

Sri Aurobindo, *Rebirth and Karma*, Section II, Chapter 15, Mind Nature and Law of Karma, pp. 128-129

The Mind's Impact on Vital Existence

In order to understand the mental energy as it manifests in the world, it is essential to look at its varying types of effort and impacts. The first, and most familiar to us, is the impact, influence and control the mental energy exercises on the physical and vital life. The power of mentality is at work, but the purpose, goal and focus is on achieving the aims of the vital life force. If we look at the characterisation made by ancient seers and sages, this would encompass the first two of the four goals or aspects they attribute as meaning to human existence, namely, *artha* and *kama*, the seeking and attainment of profit and fulfillment of desire.

The powers of mind concentrated on the achievement of these aims can be extremely powerful and can lead to tremendous success along these lines, but it is a success that remains quite limited and does not represent the power of mentality carrying out its own native lines of action. It is an important step for the transformation away from the purely animal existence, but it does not represent the true larger role that mentality is intended to play.

Sri Aurobindo discusses this aspect of mentality: "The mind no doubt feeds its powers on the effort and its fullness on the prize, but it is tethered to its pasture. It is a mixed movement, mental in its means, predominantly vital in its returns; its standard of the values of the return are measured by an outward success and failure, an externalised or externally caused pleasure and suffering, good fortune and evil fortune, the fate of the life and the body. It is this powerful vital preoccupation which has given us one element of the current notion of law of Karma, its idea of an award of vital happiness and suffering as the measure of cosmic justice."

Sri Aurobindo, *Rebirth and Karma*, Section II, Chapter 15, Mind Nature and Law of Karma, pp. 129-130

The Development of the Concept of Moral and Ethical Law

As the human mind develops beyond its first focus on purely vital success and fulfillment, we see the next stage as the attempt to abstract out of the life experience some basic principles or rules which get framed into the concept of "right", which became in the ancient Indian philosophy, the concept known as "Dharma". We see here a more characteristically mental framework developing an independence from the needs for vital success in life, and a corresponding attempt to control life based on these abstract principles.

Sri Aurobindo describes the evolutionary position of the concept of Dharma: "The idea of Dharma is on the contrary predominantly moral in its essence. Dharma on its heights holds up the moral law in its own right and for its own sake to human acceptance and observance. The larger idea of Dharma is indeed a conception of the true law of all energies and includes a conscience, a rectitude in all things, a right law of thought and knowledge, of aesthesis, of all other human activities and not only of our ethical action. But yet in the notion of Dharma the ethical element has tended always to predominate and even to monopolise the concept of Right which man creates,—because ethics is concerned with action of life and his dealing with his vital being and with his fellow men and that is always his first preoccupation and his most tangible difficulty, and because here first and most pressingly the desires, interests, instincts of the vital being find themselves cast into a sharp and very successful conflict with the ideal of Right and the demand of the higher law. Right ethical action comes therefore to seem to man at his stage the one thing binding upon him among the many standards raised by the mind, the moral claim the one categorical imperative, the moral law the whole of his Dharma."

We see here a real transition from the non-moral law of the vital world, and the first mental developments focused on supporting and achieving success in the world of life and action, to a more purely mental framework that seeks to modify life, and impose itself regardless of the vital desires and fulfillments. Of course, this starts out as a mixed action still highly colored by the desires, demands and needs of the vital being of man, and thus, the ideals and goals set in this initial stage are very much vital goals.

Sri Aurobindo, *Rebirth and Karma*, Section II, Chapter 15, Mind Nature and Law of Karma, pp. 130-131

The Current Notions of the Law of Karma

As the mental force begins to make itself felt and tries to develop a law or rule of life, it starts out with the demands, needs, desires and fears of the dynamic life force as the primary controlling factor with which it has to grapple. Rather than being able to impose, therefore, a reasoned moral and ethical code, it resorts to attempts to modify and upgrade the vital impetus through offering a system of rewards and punishments, a "carrot and a stick", for following the basic lines set forth in the moral doctrines. On close examination it can be seen that even the goals set forth at this point are mostly driven by the vital drive for success, achievement and prosperity and the fear of loss, suffering and pain.

It is thus at this point that the most common ideas about the law of Karma appear and take center stage. The moral principle, the ethical ideal is tied to the concept that the "good" will achieve worldly success; or if not worldly success, then at least a success in a life hereafter. The influence of the vital power is clearly seen in the fact that "right" has to be tied to "success" in order to be something to be attempted.

Sri Aurobindo describes this situation as follows: "It is these notions, this idea of the moral law, of righteousness and justice as a thing in itself imperative, but still needing to be enforced by bribe and menace on our human nature,–which would seem to show that at least for that nature they are not altogether imperative,–this insistence on reward and punishment because morality struggling with our first unregenerate being has to figure very largely as a mass of restraints and prohibitions and these cannot be enforced without some fact or appearance of a compelling or inducing outward sanction, this diplomatic compromise or effort at equivalence between the impersonal ethical and the personal egoistic demand, this marriage of convenience between right and vital utility, virtue and desire,–it is these accommodations that are embodied in the current notions of the law of Karma."

Sri Aurobindo, *Rebirth and Karma*, Section II, Chapter 15, Mind Nature and Law of Karma, pp. 131-132

Morality and the Vital Force

The mental force interacts with the physical world and the vital force to create a "mixed" action. This action can enhance the results achieved by the vital force. It can also interject mental principles into the action that can begin to add a moral or ethical element to the striving of the vitality. Morality is not a principle of the vital force, per se. As has been discussed previously, the fruits of success in the vital action go to those who have the best understanding, strength and conditions for that success. The advent of mentality adds another condition or element to the striving for success, by creating moral or ethical rules which create a framework within which the vital force is then permitted to operate. This does not mean, however, that the distinction between the mental force's action and the results on the vital level can be blurred or glossed over. The mixing of the mental and vital yields a much more nuanced and complex result.

Sri Aurobindo delves into this issue: "At first sight, if success is the desideratum, it is not clear what morality has to say in the affair, since we see in most things that it is a right understanding and intelligent or intuitive practice of the means and conditions and an insistent power of the will, a settled drive of the force of the being of which success is the natural consequence. Man may impose by a system of punishments a check on the egoistic will and intelligence in pursuit of its vital ends, may create a number of moral conditions for the world's prizes, but this might appear, as is indeed contended in certain vitalistic theories, an artificial imposition on Nature and a dulling and impoverishment of the free and powerful play of the mind force and the life force in their alliance. But in truth the greatest force for success is a right concentration of energy, *tapasya*, and there is an inevitable moral element in Tapasya."

Sri Aurobindo, *Rebirth and Karma*, Section II, Chapter 15, Mind Nature and Law of Karma, pp. 132-133

The Foundations For Development of Morality and Ethics as Powers In Life

As the mental power works to gain control over the vital energy, there has to be a shift from the instinctive action of the vital to a more free exercise of the will. This provides both more scope for development and more need of discipline and restraint in order to direct and manage the energy effectively. The mental power includes morality and ethics as one of its lines, but these are not sole and fully determinative as there are actually a number of factors involved in achieving result in the world of action, and the moral force is just one of them.

Sri Aurobindo explains: "The moral is not the sole element: it is not entirely true that the moral right always prevails or that where there is the dharma, on that side is the victory. The immediate success often goes to other powers, even an ultimate conquest of the Right comes usually by an association with some form of Might."

The concept of morality does play a part, especially in the interactions in society where we need the cooperation and good will of others, and the support of the framework of organisation of the nation and machinery of government in order to succeed. In this instance, any willful disregard of the moral aspect can lead to opposition and cross-currents that would inevitably weaken, or even defeat the goal of the effort. As a result there are automatically checks that make it difficult for someone to use the mental power to gain control over the vital and physical life to an extreme degree.

"Moreover, man in the use of his energies has to take into account of his fellows and the aid and opposition of their energies, and his relations with them impose on him checks, demands and conditions which have or evolve a moral significance. There is laid on him almost from the first a number of obligations even in the pursuit of vital success and satisfaction which become a first empirical basis of an ethical order."

Sri Aurobindo, *Rebirth and Karma*, Section II, Chapter 15, Mind Nature and Law of Karma, pp. 133-134

The Jealousy of the Gods

As we exercise our mental powers and will to achieve vital success in the world, we not only have to face the resistances stemming from our physical and vital nature, and the response of others with whom we interact and the social organization within which we move, but we also have to face a universal or cosmic force of evolutionary intention and development. This force essentially maintains the basic principles or laws of the universal manifestation, whether we understand or recognize them or not. While we may experience this in our lives, and talk of it as "luck" or "fate" or "necessity", we do not often focus on or pay attention to this force and its operation.

Sri Aurobindo points out that the ancient Greeks had a great appreciation for this force and its operation on our lives and our destiny. It is "a Power that is on the watch for man in his effort at enlargement, possession and enjoyments and seems hostile and opposite. The Greeks figured it as the jealousy of the gods or as Doom, Necessity, Ate. The egoistic force in man may proceed far in its victory and triumph, but it has to be wary or it will find this power there on the watch for any flaw in his strength or action, any sufficient opportunity for his defeat and downfall. It dogs his endeavour with obstacle and reverse and takes advantage of his imperfections, often dallying with him, giving him long rope, delaying and abiding its time,–and not only of his moral shortcomings but of his errors of will and intelligence, his excesses and deficiencies of strength and prudence, all defects of his nature."

This force tends to moderate the extremes. As we become more successful we tend to become arrogant and exercise our power in ever more extreme manifestations–until this force brings us back into balance and forces us to achieve the balance that our own striving and ambition blinded us from seeing. The Greeks held this to be the action of the gods. Today we may recognise a basic law of equilibrium or homeostasis that maintains the order of the universe and only permits change and development if it adheres to the universal principles and meets with the needs of the time spirit. Individual effort and success must be tempered by a sense of the Oneness and a balance in our proceeding. That is why "the Greeks held moderation in all things to be the greatest part of virtue."

Sri Aurobindo, *Rebirth and Karma*, Section II, Chapter 15, Mind Nature and Law of Karma, pg. 134

Cosmic Law and Karma

The powerful imagery of the human transgressing limits and then being struck down by a force of cosmic justice has permeated our response to life's setbacks through the ages. We need only look to the famous ancient Greek tale of Oedipus or the story of the house of Atreus, or even tales such as Hamlet or Macbeth by Shakespeare to recognise that we have imbibed these concepts and accepted them at some level of our consciousness as "the way the universe works."

It is at this point that we generally assign a moral or ethical component to this universal action, but as Sri Aurobindo point out, the response is not strictly to moral failings but actually a response to any form of weakness, insufficiency, imperfection at whatever level it manifests. The human striving is to exceed our limits, to achieve success in life through expansion, extension and enjoyment. We push ourselves to and beyond the normal limits. To the extent we have truly understood and implemented the universal laws we achieve that success; but wherever we have any imperfection in our energy, the universe takes that into account in the response and in the result. The inter-relationship between all manifested beings and forces in the universal eco-sphere and bio-sphere is a very sensitive mechanism so our attempt to aggrandise ourselves in any way sets up waves of action that both push forward and create feedback and various forms of resistance.

Sri Aurobindo summarizes this action: "The law it represents is that our imperfections shall have their passing or their fatal consequences, that a flaw in our output of energy may be mended or counterbalanced and reduced in consequence, but if persisted in shall react even in excess of its apparent merits, that an error may seem to destroy all the result of the Tapasya, because it springs from a radical unsoundness in the intention of the will, the heart, the ethical sense or the reason. This is the first line of the transitional law of Karma."

Sri Aurobindo, *Rebirth and Karma*, Section II, Chapter 15, Mind Nature and Law of Karma, pp. 134-135

"As Ye Sow, So Shall Ye Reap"?

Sri Aurobindo brings up the phenomenon that has been so frequently the basis of the idea that there is a moral order in the universe that manages responses to our actions in some kind of relatively precise way. "For there can be distinguished in Nature a certain element of the law of the talion or–perhaps a more appropriate figure, since this action seems rather mechanical than rational and deliberate–a boomerang movement of energy returning upon its transmitter. The stone we throw is flung back by some hidden force in the world upon ourselves, the action we put out upon others recoils, not always by a direct reaction, but often by devious and unconnected routes, on our own lives and sometimes, though that is by no means a common rule, in its own exact figure or measure. This is a phenomenon so striking to our imagination and impressive to our moral sense and vital feelings that it has received some kind of solemn form and utterance in the thought of all cultures..."

At the same time, Sri Aurobindo cautions that we cannot simply adopt this rule as "sufficient evidence of a moral order." While such dramatic incidents impress us, they are neither universally occurring nor generally applicable. "If it were a regular feature, men would soon learn the code of the draconian impersonal legislator and know what to avoid and the list of life's prohibitions and vetoes. But there is no such clear penal legislation of Nature."

This retributive action, when it occurs, is more illustrative of the more general principles of the lines of energy having their own effect, and eliciting forth both forces that respond to such action and those that oppose and deny that line. Thus, those who "live by the sword" will tend to "die by the sword", not by some moral imperative of the karmic order, but because the energy they create and the efforts they make put them in the way of a response in kind.

Sri Aurobindo, *Rebirth and Karma*, Section II, Chapter 15, Mind Nature and Law of Karma, pp. 135-136

Moving Beyond the Concept of Retributive Justice

It is easy for us to believe and hope that there is some kind of judge that metes out rewards and punishments to us on our merits, and that this judge keeps a scale or balance of account for each one of us and is able to precisely return to us our "just desserts". Such a system, while satisfying to some part of our developed moral sense, does not actually work out in this kind of precise mechanical way, as the interactive forces are far too complex or this kind of simplistic model of the universe.

Sri Aurobindo has provided his insight into this question: "The mathematical precision of physical Nature's action and reaction cannot indeed be expected from mental and vital Nature. For not only does everything become infinitely more subtle, complex and variable as we rise in the scale so that in our life action there is an extraordinary intertwining of forces and mixture of many values, but, even, the psychological and moral value of the same action differs in different cases, according to the circumstance, the conditions, the motive and mind of the doer."

There have been attempts to mete out human ideas of justice in such a form as "an eye for an eye, a tooth for a tooth", but such attempts do not succeed in capturing the essence of justice nor in advancing the development of consciousness in humanity. Such a system superimposed on the universe would be bound to fail as well.

"And it is evident too that the slow, long and subtle purposes of the universal Power working in the human race would be defeated rather than served by any universality of this too precise and summary procedure."

The instances of such apparent direct return of energies expended with energies returned, when they occur, are enduring and powerful examples that we like to point to, but they do not represent a universal mechanical system but more the confluence of a number of forces reacting and responding to a specific set of circumstances. Because we do not see such a definite "cause/effect" relationship in each individual's life, we have then built up the idea of precise retribution or recompense coming to us in some future lifetime…without however the factual basis to support this kind of superstructure for the universal action. Who is it that would get the future result in that future lifetime?

How would such an action carry itself forward in the complex universal energy? Would such a response have any benefit or meaning in that future lifetime? How would it "fit" into the framework of that future life? We leave all of these, and many more, questions without any answer when we shift the result of action into some future, undefined lifetime.

Sri Aurobindo, *Rebirth and Karma*, Section II, Chapter 15, Mind Nature and Law of Karma, pg. 136

Karmic Lightning Strikes

There is a return on energy expended, but it does not always land on the specific perpetrator of the act for which the return is due. While in some cases the actual culprit gets the stroke, in other cases it can be future generations, or totally innocent bystanders who get hit by what Sri Aurobindo calls the "lightnings of a retaliatory doom."

The individual responsible for setting a certain line of action in motion may obtain the fruits of that action in the short term, while nature prepares a response that happens to hit in the next generation or later. The same may be true of nations in their collective action upon others. One day there comes the payback and individuals who had nothing at all to do with the original action find themselves caught up in the rebound of energy that simply took its own time to work itself out.

We can see here, then, the working of what Sri Aurobindo calls the second transitional law of Karma. Energy is not lost. The effect is simply not immediate nor does it precisely hit those who set the force in motion. What is missing here is our preoccupation with individual responsibility as Nature treats all energy and all action as part of a whole and visits the response upon whomever happens to be there at the moment of the rebound.

Sri Aurobindo concludes: "It is evident that we cannot make much of a force that works out in so strange a fashion, however occasionally striking and dramatic its pointing at cause and consequence. It is too uncertain in its infliction of penalty to serve the end which the human mind expects from a system of penal justice, too inscrutably variable in its incidence to act as an indicator to that element in the human temperament which waits upon expediency and regulates its steps by a prudential eye to consequence."

The lesson is sometimes clear and obvious, but since it does not fall on the perpetrator, it has a more diffuse effect to suppress the extremes of the vital arrogance in a general way.

This action "serves therefore a certain moral purpose in the will in the universe, but is not itself, even in combination with the other, sufficient to be the law of a moral order." The "other" here referred to is the force of specific retributive justice which also does not function in a precise manner satisfying to our human moral and ethical sense. We see Nature acting not on individuals, in and of themselves, but on larger movements of energy within the unified field of the manifestation. Nature does not seem to care upon whom it visits the retribution. It is truly in this sense a random "lightning strike".

Sri Aurobindo, *Rebirth and Karma*, Section II, Chapter 15, Mind Nature and Law of Karma, pp. 136-137

Life Energy Is Not Governed By a Moral Code

Many of us accept the idea that "like begets like" on the field of action. While this dictum may be true on the purely physical level of the reproduction of species, it clearly does not stand up to scrutiny when it comes to the results we see in the vital world of life. There are limited circumstances we can point to where this concept works to a certain degree, but eventually it breaks down and does not yield an overarching law or moral code that governs the universe.

Sri Aurobindo examines this question: "In the terms of a moral return or rather repayment to moral energies this would mean that by putting forth love we get a return of love and by putting forth hatred a return of hatred, that if we are merciful or just to others, others also will be to us just or merciful and that generally good done by us to our fellow-men will return in a recompense of good done by them in kind and posted back to our address duly registered in the moral post office of the administrative government of the universe."

Certainly from the individual viewpoint trying to find out a rule of life, there is a certain amount of value in such a concept, to the extent that when we put out positive, warm, loving, supportive energies, we tend to create positive responses in many cases, just as when we put out angry, hateful energies, we tend to elicit angry and hateful replies. The problem with this approach is that it is clearly not universal and thus, we can just as easily point to circumstances where evil repaid good, or where being compassionate did not lead to a return in kind. How else can we explain the crucifixion of Jesus, or the Nazi holocaust? We see the strong and powerful prosper, without regard for moral right or wrong. If they calibrate their action to avoid the most extreme responses in kind, they can maintain their position for long periods of time. "If something in the world and in man returns good for good and evil for evil, it as often returns evil for good and, with or without a conscious moral intention, good for evil." "Attila and Jenghiz on the throne to the end, Christ on the cross and Socrates drinking his portion of hemlock are no very clear evidence for any optimistic notion of a law of moral return in the world of human nature."

The limitation here is that the vital world of life is not strictly organised on "moral" or "ethical" principles and thus, we cannot really expect that these principles will govern life action in its entirety.

Sri Aurobindo, *Rebirth and Karma*, Section II, Chapter 15, Mind Nature and Law of Karma, pp. 137-139

The Foundations of a Moral Order in Life

The idea that moral good is linked to achievement of success in the vital world of the life energy is one that has limited applicability, and that primarily through an indirect influence based on one type of energy interacting with another. Sri Aurobindo explains: "…because good and evil are moral and not vital values and have a clear right only to a moral and not a vital return, because reward and punishment put forward as the conditions of good doing and evil doing do not constitute and cannot create a really moral order, the principle itself, whatever temporary end it serves, being fundamentally immoral from the highest point of view of a true and pure ethics, and because there are other forces that count and have their right,–knowledge, power and many others. The correspondence of moral and vital good is a demand of the human ego and like many others of its demands answers to certain tendencies in the world mind, but is not its whole law or highest purpose."

This is not to say that there is no basis at all for morality or ethics. It is simply to help us avoid confusion between two different orders of consciousness and energy that it is important to keep a clear-sighted view of the differences between the action of energy on the vital life plane versus the energies of planes of mental energy where morality is one of the (but not the sole) principles that govern action at that level and which get their return in their own native sphere primarily.

To bring the moral order into our life and action, it is necessary to first understand this distinction, and then to exercise the influence that the moral principle can have as we enter into the field of vital expression. "A moral order there can be, but it is in ourselves and for its own sake that we have to create it and, only when we have so created it and found its right relation to other powers of life, can we hope to make it count at its full value in the right ordering of man's vital existence."

Sri Aurobindo, *Rebirth and Karma*, Section II, Chapter 15, Mind Nature and Law of Karma, pp. 139-140

SECTION III

THE HIGHER LINES OF KARMA

CHAPTER SIXTEEN

THE HIGHER LINES OF KARMA

16

The Mental Being's Adventure of Consciousness In Life

Humanity represents the development of a mental being active in the vital functions of life in the physical world. The first expressions of mentality are primarily focused on enhancing the experience of life, on achieving goals of success and rewards for mastering the physical and vital energies. However, this does not represent the essential nature of the mental being.

Sri Aurobindo describes the characteristics of mental nature: "The innate demand of the mental being is for mental experience, for the mind's manifold strengths, its capacities, joys, growth, perfections, and for these things for their own sake because of the inevitable satisfaction they give to his nature,–the demand of the intellect for truth and knowledge, the demand of the ethical mind for right and good, the demand of the aesthetic mind for beauty and delight of beauty, the demand of the emotional mind for love and the joy of relation with our fellow-beings, the demand of the will for self-mastery and mastery of things and the world and our existence. And the values which the mental being holds for supreme and effective are the values of truth and knowledge, of right and good, of beauty and aesthetic delight, of love and emotional joy, of mastery and inner lordship. It is these things that he seeks to know and follow, to possess, discover, enjoy, increase. It is for this great adventure that he came into the world, to walk hardily through the endless fields they offer to him, to experiment, to dare, to test the utmost limit of each capacity and follow each possibility and its clue to the end as well as to observe in each its at present discovered law and measure."

The foundation, basis and purpose of the mental being takes place outside the needs and demands of the physical being and the vital life of desire in the world. The mental sphere is the first one that can separate itself from the business of life and thus, is the first one that admits a true principle of morality or ethics not based on the negotiation implicit in the "reward and punishment" model. And thus, in terms of our review of the law of Karma, we may expect to see karmic consequence and returns on the mental plane that do not necessarily involve success or failure in terms of vital life rewards or physical well-being.

Sri Aurobindo, *Rebirth and Karma*, Section III, Chapter 16, The Higher Lines of Karma, pp. 143-144

Discovering Our Hidden Secret Link To the Infinite

When mind-nature separates itself from the physical and vital preoccupations, it can begin to focus on and develop itself along the lines of the mental force in its native, pure form. This does not, in and of itself, overcome the natural tendencies of the physical and the vital levels of being. There can result several lines of action. One of these develops more or less pure forms of mental activity essentially divorced from life, action and the needs of the physical nature. Another attempts to bring about modifications to the life of the world through what is essentially a process of compromise, whereby mental principles are adapted and watered down such that they can have an influence and positive effect on the energies of life in the material world, while life processes are uplifted and transformed by this new, higher influence.

Sri Aurobindo recognizes the need to bring the mental influence into the world, "...for it is by that effort that he is man and not the animal and without it he cannot find his true satisfaction in living."

At the same time, he also recognizes that mental nature, in order to fulfill its higher goals and aspirations, needs to begin to follow the principles inherent in mental nature for their own sake, and not solely for the impact they can have on a worldly life. "In other words he passes from the practical pursuit of a serviceable knowledge, morality, aesthesis, force of emotion and will-power,—serviceable for his vital aims, for life as it first is,—to an ideal pursuit of these things and the transformation of life into the image of his ideal."

Eventually as this pursuit continues, and the higher principles become more clear and defined in their form, their native form and power are unveiled, and it becomes possible to recognize what Sri Aurobindo calls the secret of human life. "There is so a chance of his discovering that as the beauty and irrefragable order of life and matter are due to the joy of the Infinite in life and in matter and the fidelity of the Force here at work to the hidden knowledge and will and idea of the Self and Spirit in them, so there is within his hidden self, his own vast and covert spirit a secret of the Infinite's self-knowledge, will, joy, love and delight, mastery, right and truth of joy and action by which his own greater life rising above the vital and mental limitations can discover an infinite perfection and beauty and delight in itself and spontaneous irrefragable order."

Sri Aurobindo, *Rebirth and Karma*, Section III, Chapter 16, The Higher Lines of Karma, pp. 144-145

Mind Nature and the Moral Principle

It is at the level of mental energy that we can recognize the moral principle in its true and pure sense, not watered-down by the type of compromises that arise under the banner of morality in the world of life action. This moral principle is not based on the seeking for or achievement of rewards in life, or on the avoidance of pain and suffering in life. Rather, it is something that is sought solely on its own behalf, as something that is right and true and which fulfills the "categorical imperative" that the principle holds on the mental plane.

The karmic return achieved by following this principle is not any longer the achievements of wealth, physical well-being, or social status and respect; rather, it is the growth of the soul.

Sri Aurobindo elucidates this further: "Mounting here the ethical mind no longer follows good for a reward now on earth or in another existence, but for the sake of good, and no longer shuns evil for fear of punishment on earth later on in this life or else in another life or in hell, but because to follow evil is a degradation and affliction of its being and a fall from its innate and imperative endeavor. This is to it a necessity of its moral nature, a truly categorical imperative, a call that in the total more complex nature of man may be dulled or suppressed or excluded by the claim of its other parts and their needs, but to the ethical mind is binding and absolute."

Traditional morality, relying on reward and punishment, is a low-burning flame that is subject to being smothered by the demands of life situations and can even be seen as an obstacle to the establishment of a true morality based on the principle, not on some temporary accommodation. "Whatever its practical utility or service as a step of the transition, the mental habit of confusion and vitalistic compromise it fosters and the more questionable confusions and compromises that habit favours, have made conventional morality one of the chief of the forces that hold back human life from progressing to a true ethical order. If humanity has made any lasting and true advance, it has been not through the virtue created by reward and punishment or any of the sanctions powerful on the little vital ego, but by an insistence from the higher mind on the lower, an insistence on right for its own sake, on imperative moral values, on an absolute law and truth of ethical being and ethical conduct that must be obeyed whatever the recalcitrances of the lower mind, whatever the pains of the vital problem, whatever the external result, the inferior issue."

Sri Aurobindo, *Rebirth and Karma*, Section III, Chapter 16, The Higher Lines of Karma, pp. 145-146

The Higher Principles of Truth, Justice, Love and Compassion

We have a few legendary stories of individuals who followed a moral code, not as part of a compromise with the life principle or as a seeking for a higher reward, but for its own sake as an independent standard that needed to be carried out, for its own sake. This is an indication of the higher mental development striving to manifest in the world. When we hear the legends, we may reflect on how far distant and unattached to the values of daily living, the striving for survival, for success, for achievement, for recognition, such an ideal response actually is. Sri Aurobindo reminds us of some of these legendary individuals: "Harischandra sacrificing self and wife and child and kingdom and subjects in an unswerving fidelity to the truth of the spoken word, Shivi giving his flesh to the hawk rather than fall from his kingly duty of protection to the fugitive, the Bodhisattwa laying his body before the famished tiger, images in which sacred or epic legend has consecrated this greater kind of virtue, illuminate an elevation of the ethical will and a law of moral energy that asks for no return from man or living thing or from the gods of Karma, lays down no conditions, makes no calculation of consequence, of less or more or of the greatest good of the greatest number, admits neither hedonistic nor the utilitarian measure, but does simply the act as the thing to be done because it is right and virtue and therefore the very law of being of the ethical man, the categorical imperative of his nature."

Such an approach, if it is based on an external moral code, can become narrow and judgmental, as we have seen through time in events such as the Holy Inquisition, where the pure ethical sense is turned into an unswerving creed used to dominate and control others, in what then becomes a fanatic and one-sided view of life. Even this approach shows the underlying striving for something pure and true, however.

Sri Aurobindo advises us of the need for a true and living response based on our inner being: "No rule imposed on him from outside, whether in the name of a supposed mechanical or impersonal law or of God or prophet, can be, as such, true or right or binding on man: it becomes that only when it answers to some demand or aids some evolution of his inner being. And when that inner being is revealed, evolved, at each moment naturally active, simply and spontaneously imperative, then we get the true, the inner and intuitive Law in its light of self-knowledge, its beauty of self-fulfilment, its intimate life significance. An act of justice, truth, love, compassion, purity, sacrifice becomes then the faultless expression, the natural outflowering of our soul of justice, our soul of truth, our soul of love and compassion, our soul of purity or sacrifice."

This connects us to the higher realms of the Infinite.

Sri Aurobindo, *Rebirth and Karma*, Section III, Chapter 16, The Higher Lines of Karma, pp. 146-147

Karma Is a Law of Spiritual Evolution

As we have seen the inadequacy of any concept of Karma that reduces it to some kind of reward and punishment system based on the expectations and desires of the vital life energy, it becomes relevant to ask what, then, is the law of Karma, and how does it relate to the higher energies of mental nature and beyond.

Sri Aurobindo's response: "Meanwhile we get the clue to the higher law of Karma, of the output and returns of energy, and see it immediately and directly to be, what all law of Karma, really and ultimately, if at first covertly, is for man, a law of his spiritual evolution."

He continues: "The true return to the act of virtue, to the ethically right output of his energy–his reward, if you will, and the sole recompense on which he has a right to insist,–is its return upon him in a growth of the moral strength within him, an upbuilding of his ethical being, a flowering of the soul of right, justice, love, compassion, purity, truth, strength, courage, self-giving that he seeks to be. The true return to the act of evil, to the ethically wrong output of energy–his punishment, if you will, and the sole penalty he has any need or right to fear,–is its return upon him in a retardation of the growth, a demolition of the upbuilding, an obscuration, tarnishing, impoverishing of the soul, of the pure, strong and luminous being that he is striving to be."

Once we move our awareness and effort to the planes of mental energy, the rewards and punishments of worldly success and failure lose their attraction. Each output of energy calls forth a precise response in kind. Our focus on vital success and failure leads to results in the field of life. Our focus on the higher principles of the mental world yield results on their native plane. Influence and interchange between the different orders of energy can and do occur, and we thus can see that the strengthening of the impulses of the higher mental energies will inevitably have some impact on the world of life and action; however, the true karmic response still occurs at the level of the native energy. This explains to us why we see situations where the good are suffering in the world while the evil appear to be prospering. The inner spiritual evolution provides us the solution for why a soul, focused on increasing the principles of ethics, love, compassion, knowledge or justice may wind up accepting limitations in life for the sake of the higher principle.

"What to this high seeker of Right can mean the vital law of Karma or what can its gods do to him that he can fear or long for? The ethical-vitalistic explanation of the world and its meaning and measures has for such a soul, for man at this height of his evolution no significance."

Sri Aurobindo, *Rebirth and Karma*, Section III, Chapter 16, The Higher Lines of Karma, pg. 148

The Highest Law of Our Nature

It is a quite natural tendency of human nature to fixate on one issue to the exclusion of others. The mind, as a dividing and analyzing instrument, tends toward exclusive concentration. So it is easy to understand that when we once focus on the ethical principle, that it may be viewed as the "categorical imperative" of our human nature.

Sri Aurobindo acknowledges the role of the ethical principle, but he also puts it in context with other aspects of our nature that equally call for fulfillment. There are the seeking for knowledge, the seeking for beauty and harmony, the seeking for Oneness which also represent aspects of our nature.

Sri Aurobindo takes up this question: "The Indian thinkers had a wiser sight who while conceding right ethical being and conduct as a first need, still considered knowledge to be the greater ultimate demand, the indispensable condition, and much nearer to a full seeing came that larger experience of theirs that either through an urge towards absolute knowledge or a pure impersonality of the will or an ecstasy of divine love and absolute delight,–and even through an absorbing concentration of the psychical and the vital and physical being,–the soul turns towards the Supreme and that on each part of our self and nature and consciousness there can come a call and irresistible attraction of the Divine. Indeed, an uplift of all these, an imperative of the Divine upon all the ways of our being, is the impetus of self-enlargement to a complete, an integralising possession of God, freedom and immortality, and that therefore is the highest law of our nature."

Sri Aurobindo, *Rebirth and Karma*, Section III, Chapter 16, The Higher Lines of Karma, pp. 148-149

An Inner and Absolute Divine Imperative

The development of a moral principle in life comes about as the mental energy begins to manifest and interact with the vital energy, which in and of itself, does not have any kind of moral imperative. This concept, however, is limited by the fact that the vital fulfillment remains the pre-eminent need and goal of the vital manifestation, and the influence of this mental principle is circumscribed within limits that allow the vital achievements to proceed. As a result, the application of morality or ethics begins with ways of training, guiding or directing the vital energy rather than with the more advanced ideal conceptualization that the higher mind would like to adopt.

Sri Aurobindo discusses the limitations of the resultant compromises: "What the natural egoistic man obeys most rigorously is the collective or social rule of conduct impressed on his mind by law and tradition, jus, mores, and outside its conventional circle he allows himself an easy latitude. The reason generalizes the idea of a moral law carrying with it an obligation man should heed and obey but may disregard at this outer or that inner peril, and it insists first and most on a moral law, an obligation of self-control, justice, righteousness, conduct, rather than a law of truth, beauty and harmony, love, mastery, because the regulation of his desires and instincts and his outward vital action is his first necessary preoccupation and he has to find his poise here and a settled and sanctioned order before he commences securely to go deeper and develop more in the direction of his inner being."

As the higher mind gains more control and manifests itself more securely, we see a shifting of the focus towards the more ideal principles and a subsequent reduction in the focus on achievement of success in vital or materialistic terms. At this level, however, it is not solely a moral or ethical ideal that is called forth, as there are other aspects of the higher mentality that also need to be realized, such as "truth, beauty, love, strength and power are after all as necessary for the true growth of mind and of life and even for the fullness of the action as righteousness, purity and justice. Arriving on the high ideal plane these too become, no less than the ethical motive, no longer a seeking and necessity of this relative nature and importance, but a law and call to spiritual perfection, an inner and absolute divine imperative."

Sri Aurobindo, *Rebirth and Karma*, Section III, Chapter 16, The Higher Lines of Karma, pp. 149-150

The Development of the Power of Knowledge

The integration of the mental energy into the world of life follows a similar model to the integration of the life energy into matter. There is an initial stirring of the mental force, a reaching out, an inquisitive seeking, an attempt to understand the framework within which it is enclosed and the way its power can be exercised successfully. Subsequently, we see the mental energy engaging with the world of life and matter, gaining a deeper understanding of their functioning and beginning to exercise an increasing measure of influence or even control in that field. It is at this stage that the mental energy begins to provide serious returns in the form of more precise and powerful action, and, to the extent the life energy and physical matter have been properly understood, at least to some degree, a more successful result.

It is after the mental energy has engaged in this way that it begins to create for itself a uniquely mental space in which it can organize and express itself without concerning itself directly with the affairs of the world, and it is at this point that we see the functioning of the truly mental force in its native power and energetic action.

All along the way we see the basic principle at work that the greater the mental energy, the more knowledge is applied to the life efforts and the world repays this with results. In fact, the power of applied knowledge shows a much greater and more direct payback than other mental forces such as the moral or ethical energy that also stems from the mental realm.

Sri Aurobindo draws the following conclusions on this point: "In this material world it is at least doubtful how far moral good is repaid by vital good and moral evil punished by a recoil, but it is certain that we do pay very usually for our errors, for stupidity, for ignorance of the right way of action, for any ignoring or misapplication of the laws that govern our psychical, vital and physical being; it is certain that knowledge is a power for life efficiency and success. Intelligence pays its way in the material world, guards itself against vital and physical suffering, secures its vital rewards more surely than moral right and ethical purpose."

Sri Aurobindo, *Rebirth and Karma*, Section III, Chapter 16, The Higher Lines of Karma, pp. 150-151

The Evolution of Consciousness Involved In Life

Sri Aurobindo places the seeking for knowledge as a central aspect of the deeper intention of the universal manifestation: "The pursuit of knowledge for the sake of knowledge is the true, the intrinsic dharma of the intellect and not for the sake primarily or even necessarily at all for the securing or the enlargement of the means of life and success in action."

For most people, still rooted primarily in the vital striving for growth, expansion, aggrandizement and increase of scope and power of the life energy, this seeking of the intellect is both somewhat foreign and more or less secondary. Any action of intellect that does not seem to have a "practical" purpose may be acknowledged and accepted, but it is treated as an ornament by these individuals, not as a central purpose of life.

There is however a deeper and more essential movement of consciousness at work here: "Nature sees and stirs from the first to a larger and more inward Will and is moved with a greater purpose, and all seeking for knowledge springs from a necessity of the mind, a necessity of its nature, and that means a necessity of the soul that is here in nature."

Even when we are focused on and even preoccupied with the use of the intellect for purposes of life-aggrandizement, this deeper movement of nature continues to develop and grow. "....for if her first dynamic word is life, her greater revealing word is consciousness and the evolution of life and action only the means of the evolution of consciousness involved in life, the imprisoned soul, the Jiva. Action is a means, but knowledge is the sign and the growth of the conscious soul is the purpose."

It is the seeking for knowledge that distinguishes mankind from the other beings in the evolution of life. "Man's use of the intelligence for the pursuit of knowledge is therefore that which distinguishes him most from other beings and gives him his high peculiar place in the scale of existence. His passion for knowledge, first world-knowledge, but afterwards self-knowledge and that in which both meet and find their common secret, God-knowledge, is the central drift of his ideal mind and a greater imperative of his being than that of action, though later in laying its complete hold on him, greater in the wideness of its reach and greater too in its effectiveness upon action, in the returns of the world energy to his power of the truth within him."

Sri Aurobindo, *Rebirth and Karma*, Section III, Chapter 16, The Higher Lines of Karma, pp. 151-152

The Scientist, the Philosopher and the Sage

There comes a stage when the mental being no longer focuses its efforts on achieving success or results on the vital plane in the physical world; rather, it is focused on a seeking for Truth, for Knowledge, for some higher Absolute that answers to its deepest inner calling, regardless of the result that may be achieved by the actual application or utility of the knowledge obtained.

We can see this type develop and take various forms. The pure scientist, with an inner drive to understand the workings of the universe is one such type. The pure thinker or philosopher represents another manifestation of this same higher seeking. The tradition of the yogin, the seer, the sage, abandoning material wealth and prosperity for a higher seeking of what is "beyond" represents yet another.

In his magnum opus, The Life Divine , Sri Aurobindo sets forth in the very first chapter the "human aspiration" for "God, Light, Freedom, Immortality." This ultimate aspiration is a manifestation of the pure expression of the inner drive to obtain Knowledge.

The relevance to the question of Karma is that the return obtained by such a seeker has clearly nothing to do with reward or punishment in this life or hereafter, but with a return of greater knowledge and an experience of Oneness that results. "The lure of an external utility ceases to be at all needed as an incentive towards knowledge, just as the lure of a vital reward offered now or hereafter ceases on the same high level of our ascent to be needed as an incentive to virtue, and to attach importance to it under whatever specious colour is even felt to be a degradation of the disinterestedness, a fall from the high purity of the soul motive."

There are various stages of this higher seeking, such as the scientist's cold intellectual endeavor, or the inner drive or passion for an ultimate Truth. The common thread between them however is their lack of concern for the ordinary view of Karma and consequence. We see here the working of a higher order of the law of Karma, focusing on providing a return on the energy put out without an attempt at tying it to moral or ethical result or relevance.

Sri Aurobindo, *Rebirth and Karma*, Section III, Chapter 16, The Higher Lines of Karma, pp. 152-153

Karmic Consequence of the Soul's Seeking For Knowledge

Every energy in the universe has its "cause and effect" aspect, and thus, we can expect that there is a karmic consequence to the impulse that turns the seeking for knowledge, light, truth, God, into an imperative of the soul. As we have seen in other instances, the karmic impact of each energy is primarily focused on the plane and to the type of energy that is involved, even if there are tangential or secondary effects that take place across other types of energy.

Sri Aurobindo focuses on this issue: "But the result that it brings on this higher plane of the seeking in mind is simply and purely the upward growth of the soul in light and truth; that and whatever happiness it brings is the one supreme reward demanded by the soul of knowledge and the darkening of the light within, the pain of the fall from truth, the pain of the imperfection of not living only by its law and wholly in the light is its one penalty of suffering. The outward rewards and the sufferings of life are small things to the higher soul of knowledge in man: even his high mind of knowledge will often face all that the world can do to afflict it, just as it is ready to make all manner of sacrifices in the pursuit and the affirmation of the truth it knows and lives for."

One cannot expect that the intense drive that motivates an individual to place the pursuit of knowledge as the highest goal and aspiration is going to yield rewards of physical comfort, vital satisfaction or some kind of success in the world as its ordinary result. This illustrates the basic principle that Sri Aurobindo has described that untangles the normal view of karma to show that specific types of energy do not tend to provide clear results of another and different type. Just as the focus on vital success in life, the accumulation of wealth and material comfort is not tied, one way or the other, to moral or ethical focus in the being, so the "rewards and punishments" that are attendant on the seeking for pure knowledge must necessarily be primarily related to the mental and spiritual energies being put forth in that seeking.

Sri Aurobindo, *Rebirth and Karma*, Section III, Chapter 16, The Higher Lines of Karma, pp. 153-154

The Spiritual Justification and Intention of Nature

The solution to the riddle of rebirth and karma lies in understanding of the secret intention that is working itself out through these mechanisms. Sri Aurobindo reviews this intention: "At first she is physical Nature building her firm field according to a base of settled truth and law but determined by a subconscient knowledge she does not yet share with her creatures. Next she is Life growing slowly self-conscious, seeking out knowledge that she may move seeingly in them along her ways and increase at once the complexity and the efficacy of her movements, but developing slowly too the consciousness that knowledge must be pursued for a higher and purer end, for truth, for the satisfaction, as the life expression and as the spiritual self-finding of the soul of knowledge. But, last, it is that soul itself growing in truth and light, growing into the absolute truth of itself which is its perfection, that becomes the law and high end of her energies."

Each of these stages has a characteristic type of energy that is expressed, and the return for that energy is correlated to that characteristic type. Thus, we see that the law of Karma varies in its expression depending on the type of energy. "At first there is the return of skill and effectual intelligence–and her own need explains sufficiently why she gives the rewards of life not, as the ethical mind in us would have it, to the just, not chiefly to moral good, but to the skilful and to the strong, to will and force and intelligence,–and then, more and more clearly disengaged, the return of enlightenment and the satisfaction of the mind and the soul in the conscious use and wise direction of its powers and capacities and, last of all, the one supreme return, the increase of the soul in light, the satisfaction of is perfection in knowledge, its birth into the highest consciousness and the pure fulfilment of its own innate imperative. It is that growth, a divine birth or spiritual self-exceeding its supreme reward, which for the eastern mind has been always the highest gain,–the growth out of human ignorance into divine self-knowledge."

We can see in this schema that the confused ideas about the law of Karma prevalent in our normal line of understanding can be disentangled and put into a perspective which reveals a systematic, step-by-step development with the energies of the world precisely responding to the level and intensity of the energy that we expend in the world.

Sri Aurobindo, *Rebirth and Karma*, Section III, Chapter 16, The Higher Lines of Karma, pg. 154

Appendix I

The Tangle of Karma

Spiritual Truth Vs. Mechanical Law

The usual conceptions of the law of Karma revolve around either the sense that there is some machinery that metes out precise responses to our actions; or else, that there is some tribunal somewhere that weighs and metes out rewards and punishments to us based on those deeds. Sri Aurobindo, however, has indicated that the truth behind the action is far more complex, as well as far more flexible than the popular concepts would acknowledge.

"No rigid narrow ethical law bound down to a petty human significance is here, no unprofitable wheel of a brutal cosmic justice automatically moved in the traces of man's ignorant judgments and earthly desires and instincts. Not these artificial constructions but a thing spiritual and intimate to the deepest intention of Nature. The ascending march of the soul's consciousness and experience as it emerges out of subconscient Matter and climbs to its own luminous divinity fixes the norm and constantly enlarges the lines of the law or let us say rather since law is too mechanical a conception the truth of Karma."

Insight into the workings of Karma requires therefore both a patient observation at the level of the physical world and the action of the life energy and mental energy and an insight based on our deeper spiritual being that is aligned with the inner sense and meaning of the universal manifestation. This in turn requires us to give up the popular framework that has acted as the definition of Karma in the past, and acknowledge that Karma is essentially the working out of the universal evolutionary energy within the limitations of each type of energy that successively manifests. It may take on the aspect of a mechanical cause and effect at the most basic levels of physical energy, but as it ascends in the scale of consciousness, it becomes ever more subtle, with actions across energy types possible, but limited by the interaction and intensity of that interaction.

Sri Aurobindo, *Rebirth and Karma*, Appendix I, The Tangle of Karma, pg. 155

A New Understanding of the Action of Karma

The basic tendency and characteristic of the mind is to divide, analyze and classify. We use this power to great advantage in our attempt to harness powers of Nature, but we must also recognize that this power has its disadvantages, particularly when we try to address the meaning of life and our own spiritual development, things which require a unifying rather than a dividing intelligence.

We have used our fragmenting and characterizing capabilities to try to understand the working of the law of Karma, but we have now had to recognize that this has led to over-simplification and, at last, to a failure to appreciate the vast, manifold and flexible movement that actually is the basis for what we call Karma.

Sri Aurobindo sets about to re-set our understanding, and thereby move us beyond the limits of the mechanical view we have had of Karma to a much more dynamic view: "Let us then call Karma no longer a Law, but rather the many-sided dynamic truth of action and life, the organic movement here of the Infinite."

"Action of Karma follows and takes up into its flexible sweep and surge many potential lines of the Spirit; it is the processus of the creative Infinite; it is the long and many-sided way of the progression of the individual and the cosmic soul in Nature. Its complexities cannot be unravelled by our physical mind ever bound up in the superficial appearance, nor by our vital mind of desire stumbling forward in the cloud of its own longings and instincts and rash determinations through the maze of the myriad favoring and opposing forces of the visible and the invisible worlds. Nor can it be perfectly classified, accounted for, tied up in bundles by the precisions of our logical intelligence in its inveterate search for clear-cut formulas."

A true understanding of Karma can only come about when we are able to see with the vision of the integrating intelligence which Sri Aurobindo has called the supramental consciousness. This consciousness holds together all the apparently opposing and disparate parts in a complex, interacting, complete Oneness while simultaneously recognising the individual strands and streams of action and manifestation.

Sri Aurobindo, *Rebirth and Karma*, Appendix I, The Tangle of Karma, pp. 155-156

Interaction of the Physical, Vital, Mental and Spiritual Lines of Energy

It is not possible to fully understand the action of Karma solely by looking at the specific lines of energy of the physical, vital, mental and supramental levels. In the world we inhabit, these are always inextricably intertwined. While specific individuals may take their stand primarily within the framework of one or another of these levels, it is nevertheless obvious that they still must take into account the impact of the others. Focusing on the mental principles, for instance, does not absolve anyone from the demands and realities of the physical body or the vital impulsions.

It is therefore important to recognize the effects of this interaction and realize that we cannot truly understand Karma by analytical abstraction. The difficulties of the attempt to integrate the higher levels of consciousness into the world dominated by the physical and the vital forces has led the spiritual seeker to attempt to cut off or abandon that outer life of action. Sri Aurobindo describes the predicament: "The moment he tries to get at the absolute of the spirit, he feels himself obliged to reject body, to silence mind, and to draw back from life. It is that urgent necessity, that inability of mind and life and body to hold and answer to the spirit that is the secret of asceticism, the philosophical justification of the illusionist, the compulsion that moves the eremite and the recluse."

The alternative is based on attempting to bring the higher forces of mind and spirit into life: "If on the other hand he tries to spiritualise mind and life and the body he finds in the end that he has only brought down the spirit to a lower formulation that cannot give all its truth and purity and power."

This has led to the degradation of these higher energies, as the lower powers clearly water down the effect of the higher in action. "He has never yet spiritualised the body, at most he has minimised the physical by a spiritual refusal and abstinence or brought down some mental and vital powers mistaken for spiritual into his physical force and physical frame."

Thus, we see the lines of Karma interwoven into a complex web of impacts that are not a straight, unbroken and direct line that can be teased out through mental process. The predominant lines must be seen, the intensity of the movement of that energy must be gauged, and the interaction with other parts of our being must be calculated to get at a more precise view of karmic action. These again must be taken in context of the larger movements of these energies across the entire world movements of energy.

Sri Aurobindo, *Rebirth and Karma*, Appendix I, The Tangle of Karma, pp. 156-158

The Supramental Consciousness
Is Key To Transcending the
Limitations of Mind, Life and Matter

The mental, vital and physical levels of consciousness are fundamentally limited by their basis in division and fragmentation. They see and categorize their understanding in a way that emphasizes the separateness of the forces at work and the consequences. This makes it impossible to understand the action of Karma in any comprehensive way, as such an understanding requires an integrating vision that can both see the parts and the whole of which they are elements.

Sri Aurobindo elucidates this point: "The secret reason of man's failure to rise truly beyond himself is a fundamental incapacity in the mind, the life and the body to organise the highest integral truth and power of the spirit. And this incapacity exists because mind and life and matter are in their nature depressed and imperfect powers of the Infinite that need to be transformed into something greater than themselves before they can escape from their depression and imperfection; in their very nature they are a system of partial and separated values and cannot adequately express or embody the integral and the one, a movement of many divergent and mutually non-understanding or misunderstanding lines they cannot arrive of themselves at any but a provisional limited and imperfect harmony and order."

To the extent that we can develop any kind of harmony of interaction, it is based on the action of the secret influence of the higher supramental consciousness which holds the whole in its vision while simultaneously recognising the role and place for each of the disparate parts.

"That force and knowledge is the self-possessed supramental power and will and the perfect and untrammelled supramental gnosis of the Infinite. It is that which has fixed the precise measures of Matter, regulates the motive instincts and impulsions of Life, holds together the myriad seekings of Mind; but none of these things are that power and gnosis and nothing therefore mental, vital or physical is final or can even find its own integral truth and harmony nor all these together their reconciliation until they are taken up and transformed in a supramental manifestation. For this supermind or gnosis is the entire organising will and knowledge of the spiritual, it is the Truth Consciousness, the Truth Force, the organic instrumentation of divine Law, the all-seeing eye of the divine Vision, the freely selecting and generating harmony of the eternal Ananda."

And it is from this standpoint that the entire process of rebirth, and the action of Karma can finally be integrated and understood, both in the individual lines of action of each level of consciousness and in the complex interaction that provides the framework for the evolutionary journey of the soul through time, space and circumstance in the manifestation of the secret meaning of existence.

Sri Aurobindo, *Rebirth and Karma*, Appendix I, The Tangle of Karma, pp. 158-159

Appendix II

Question and Answer: A Clarification

Clarifications Regarding Purusha and Prakriti In the Understanding of Karma

There is a passage in the Upanishads, relevant to the discussion of rebirth and karma, which raised a question in the mind of one of the students of Sri Aurobindo's text Rebirth and Karma. The Upanishad refers to "mind, leader of the life and body". The student wonders how the mental being can take on this central role when it is part of the manifested lower nature of body, life and mind.

Sri Aurobindo clarified that the Upanishad referred to the "manomaya purusha" and not mind in the sense of the instrumentation of nature we commonly consider to be "mind". There is a distinction of the concepts of "purusha" and "prakriti". The first is the witness consciousness, not acting but providing support and sanction. The second is nature, which acts. In this case, the Upanishad is referring to the purusha. It specifically is referring to human beings as essentially being led by their characteristic as mental beings; while animals, for instance, would be led by their characteristic as life beings, in Upanishadic terms "pranamaya purusha".

The Taittiriya Upanishad in the Brahmananda Valli goes through an extensive review of the issue, as it successively refers to a series of ever more subtle inner selves that inform and control the more external forms. There is a self of matter, which is then informed by a self of vital energy. This in turn is informed by a self of mind. The sequence continues beyond that inner self of mind. The issue here, however is not related to the matter, life energy or mind that makes up the instrumental being in nature, but an essential inner self that provides the basic "way of being" or characteristic of the being controlled by that "self".

Sri Aurobindo discusses this issue: "It is described as manomaya by the Upanishads because the psychic being is behind the veil and man being the mental being in the life and body lives in his mind and not in his psychic, so to him the manomaya purusha is the leader of the life and body,–of the psychic behind supporting the whole he is not aware or dimly aware in his best moments."

He goes on to explain that the manomaya purusha guides the human nature (prakriti) consisting of the instrumental mind, life and body. Similarly in the animal world, it would be the pranamaya purusha (the essential consciousness of the vital life energy) that would be the leader or guide for the animal nature consisting of instrumental life and body.

It is this level of subtlety and detail that has made a complete understanding of the processes and significance of Karma so mysterious and difficult to follow throughout mankind's attempts to get an overview of it.

Sri Aurobindo, *Rebirth and Karma*, Appendix I, The Tangle of Karma, pp. 160-161

CONCLUSIONS

**We have completed our review
of** *Rebirth and Karma* **by Sri Aurobindo.**

The customary view of rebirth clearly leaves much to be desired. It is based, generally, on the idea that a specific personality will be reborn, and join up with the friends and family experienced in the current birth in another lifetime. It misses the inner rationale behind the entire process of rebirth, the growth, manifestation and evolution of the soul as a spark and "representative" of the Spirit involved in Matter for the expression of ever-greater forces of consciousness.

Similarly, the customary view of karma is also clearly flawed. The idea of either a machinery that metes out precise responses to an individual's actions, or some high tribunal measuring actions and meting out justice, across this life and future lives, clearly is a distortion of the process that is truly taking place.

What we eventually see is that there is a vast intertwined movement of different forms of energies, physical, vital, mental and spiritual, each having their own characteristic power and action, but also impacting one another and creating a new result that represents the force of each line of action, but also takes into account the effect of the interaction. A cause and effect relationship exists within this framework, but not in the mechanically simplistic manner that we have tended to ascribe to it.

This process takes place, not solely on an individual basis, but also for the characteristic action of each species of being, and for the interaction between all life forms and the environment within which they live and act, and the movement of Time in the process of manifestation. We see, not a precise machinery, but a living, breathing Being manifesting through the Oneness of the universal life.

Rebirth is seen as part of a process of soul evolution. Karma as the cause and effect relationship between an output of energy and its result and the return it provides. The individual soul, as it grows and develops, through various forms and lives, is able to gain a deeper insight and understanding of the action of Karma, and thereby adjust its action to achieve the evolutionary goal of consciously integrating the spiritual consciousness into the world of mind, life and matter.

The benefit of understanding this deeper and more complex reality is that it points the way toward the spiritual evolution that is the true sense and meaning of our lives, and provides us a way to escape the artificial and limited perspectives of physical, vital and mental impulses that hamper our growth. This viewpoint also helps us to understand and reconcile the apparently incongruous results that tend to mystify us, answering the questions of why do those doing evil prosper, or why do the good suffer, by providing the context and meaning that is secretly hidden in the entire universal life.

Sri Aurobindo, *Rebirth and Karma*, Conclusions Regarding Rebirth and Karma

BIBLIOGRAPHY

Aurobindo, Sri. *Bhagavad Gita and Its Message. 1996*
ISBN: 9780941524780
Lotus Press, Twin Lakes, WI USA **www.lotuspress.com**

Aurobindo, Sri. *The Life Divine. 1990*
ISBN: 9780941524612
Lotus Press, Twin Lakes, WI, USA **www.lotuspress.com**

Aurobindo, Sri. *Rebirth and Karma. 1991*
ISBN: 9780941524636
Lotus Press, Twin Lakes, WI, USA www.lotuspress.com

Aurobindo, Sri. *The Upanishads. 1996*
ISBN: 9780914955238
Lotus Press, Twin Lakes, WI, USA **www.lotuspress.com**

Lotus Press is the US publisher of the primary writings of Sri Aurobindo. Most of the major writings are now also available on the Amazon Kindle format. Amazon provides free kindle reading apps for PC, MAC, android, iphone, ipad and a number of other devices and platforms, as well as supporting the various Kindle reader devices they have made available.

ABOUT THE AUTHOR:

Santosh Krinsky has been studying Sri Aurobindo's *The Life Divine* since he was introduced to it in 1971. After residing at Sri Aurobindo Ashram in India for part of 1973-1974, he returned to the USA where he has been involved in the distribution and eventually the publication of the major writings of Sri Aurobindo. In 1981 he founded Lotus Light Publications which eventually became Lotus Press and took up the publication of the writings of Sri M P Pandit as well as Sri Aurobindo. Lotus Press today is one of the leading publishers also in the field of Ayurveda and alternative healing modalities, including Reiki, as well as being the US publisher of Sri Aurobindo's major works.

Santosh is also one of the founders and currently the President of a non-profit organization The Institute for Wholistic Education. The Institute is dedicated to the work of integrating spirituality into daily life. Activities include various classes, meditations, and sponsoring online informational websites and blog posts. The Institute also maintains a library of more than 6000 volumes available for use by seekers and interested parties who visit the center in Wisconsin.

Santosh and his wife Karuna reside in Racine, Wisconsin.

For more information about the work you can visit the following websites:

Sri Aurobindo Information:
www.aurobindo.net

Sri M.P. Pandit Information:
www.mppandit.com

Institute for Wholistic Education:
www.wholisticinstitute.org

Lotus Press:
www.lotuspress.com

Sri Aurobindo Studies blog:
http://sriaurobindostudies.wordpress.com

Daily Twitter feed on Sri Aurobindo and Ayurveda:
www.twitter.com/santoshk1

ABOUT THE AUTHOR:

SRI AUROBINDO

Sri Aurobindo was born in Calcutta on 15 August 1872. At the age of seven he was taken to England for education. There he studied at St. Paul's School, London, and at King's College, Cambridge. Returning to India in 1893, he worked for the next thirteen years in the Princely State of Baroda in the service of the Maharaja and as a professor in Baroda College. During this period he also joined a revolutionary society and took a leading role in secret preparations for an uprising against the British Government in India.

In 1906, soon after the Partition of Bengal, Sri Aurobindo quit his post in Baroda and went to Calcutta, where he soon became one of the leaders of the Nationalist movement. He was the first political leader in India to openly put forward, in his newspaper Bande Mataram, the idea of complete independence for the country. Prosecuted twice for sedition and once for conspiracy, he was released each time for lack of evidence.

Sri Aurobindo had begun the practice of Yoga in 1905 in Baroda. In 1908 he had the first of several fundamental spiritual realisations. In 1910 he withdrew from politics and went to Pondicherry in order to devote himself entirely to his inner spiritual life and work. During his forty years in Pondicherry he evolved a new method of spiritual practice, which he called the Integral Yoga. Its aim is a spiritual realisation that not only liberates man's consciousness but also transforms his nature. In 1926, with the help of his spiritual collaborator, the Mother, he founded the Sri Aurobindo Ashram. Among his many writings are The Life Divine, The Synthesis of Yoga and Savitri. Sri Aurobindo left his body on 5 December 1950.

Major writings of Sri Aurobindo are published in the USA by Lotus Press, Twin Lakes, WI www.lotuspress.com